A DRAIN ON OUR DIGNITY

A DRAIN ON OUR DIGNITY | An Insider's Perspective

Masixole Feni

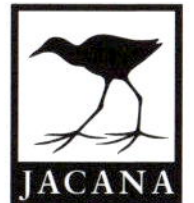

FOREWORD

Everyone has inherent dignity and the right to have their dignity respected and protected. This is what is guaranteed for everyone under section 10 of the South African Constitution. The same Constitution, as interpreted by the Constitutional Court in the Grootboom case, guarantees everyone the right to water and sanitation under section 26 (Housing).

Two decades into democracy, these rights are enjoyed by only some in South Africa, as clearly captured and documented by the brilliance of Masixole's photography. Having grown up and experienced the same indignities and injustices he documents through his photography, Masixole shows a side of Cape Town that is often hidden to the world, a side where residents are treated as second-class citizens.

Many of those living in South Africa's informal settlements and rural areas suffer daily from the indignities and injustices they experience because of the lack of access to adequate basic services, such as water and sanitation. Poor and working-class communities are still being subjected to the use of the bucket system through chemical toilets, container toilets and portable flush toilets. Many have to walk long distances to access water.

Documented here are the inequalities, class divide and the spatial injustice that our democratically elected government acknowledges but continuously fails to substantively address. These are clear when a child and her mother relieve themselves in an open field next to a national road in clear view of those driving on that road, where the majority of those driving past live in the wealthy suburbs of the same city.

A Drain on our Dignity must be viewed not just as a photo project. It must be a constant reminder that the dignity of the poor and working-class communities that are subjected to these conditions is trampled on every single day while we watch. When we are silent about what we see, we are just as bad as those we put in power who fail in their responsibility of providing basic services in an equal and just manner as envisaged by our Constitution.

Axolile Notywala
Head of Local Government Programme at Social Justice Coalition

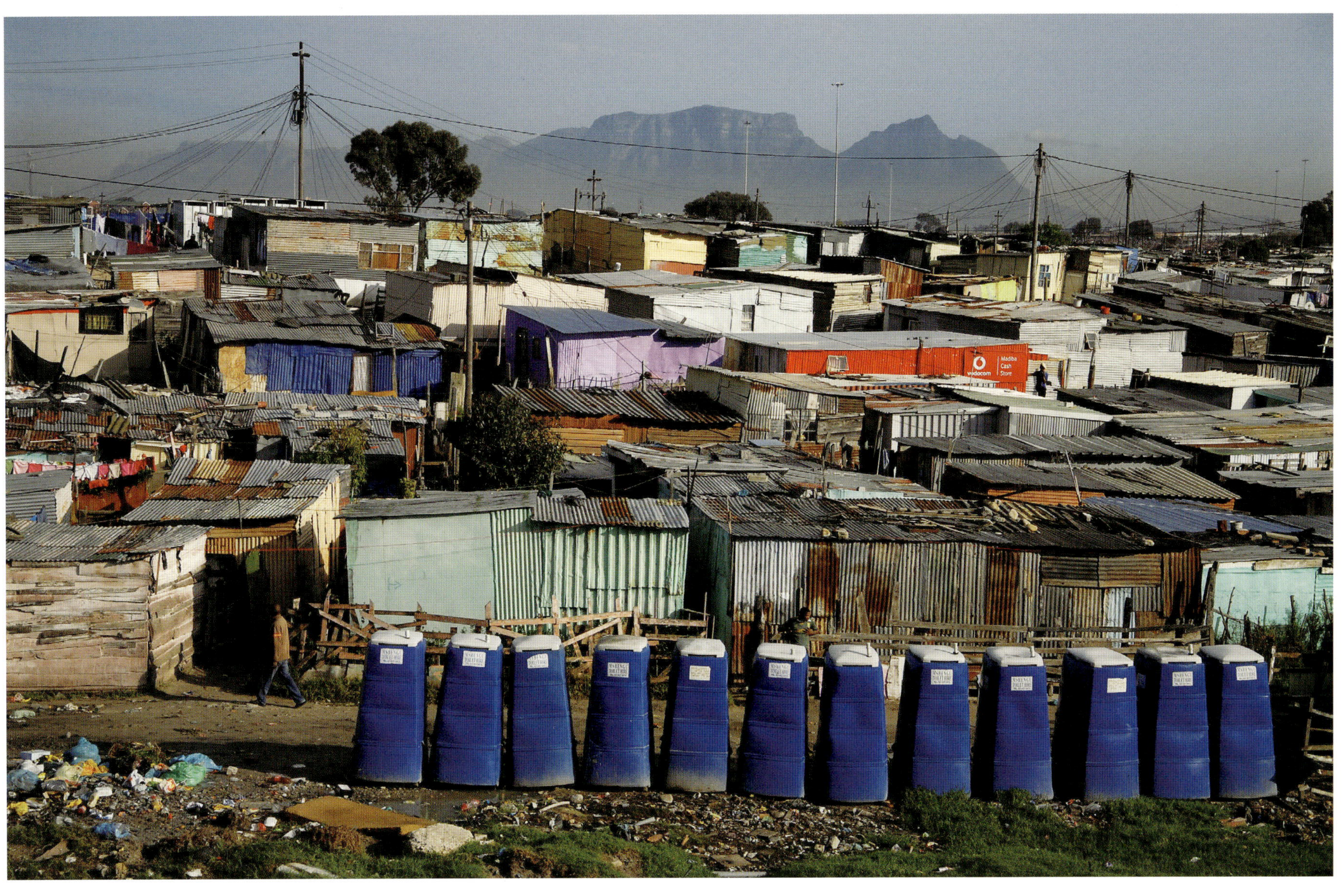

Township sanitation: A row of the Mshengu communal toilets is visible as you enter Khayelitsha.

I FIRST ENCOUNTERED Masixole Feni's photographs in GroundUp, an online news agency that reports on public-interest stories concerning governance, social movements and spatial injustice. One image stayed in my mind, powerfully, and is perhaps also a thumbnail of our long-term research collaboration. The image is of the Tafelberg school site in Sea Point, Cape Town, the site of a highly controversial development proposal between provincial government and private developers, with social housing activists pushing for the site to be allocated for conveniently located affordable housing for the poor. The headline of the article in GroundUp read: 'Tafelberg study a breakthrough, say activists. 270 units proposed for low-income households on Sea Point property.' Feni's photo that caught my attention most is a magical conflation of two very specific architectural styles – the lower half of the image is of a government-style low-maintenance brick face and the exposed concrete pavilion of the Tafelberg school. Above the pavilion, peeking over the low roof of the structure, you can see a multi-storey, tinted glass and concrete corporate-style office building. In many ways, this image captures the common tale of South African land use and development and the architecture that it produces.

For me, working in Cape Town as an architect and researcher in spatial justice, I read the contemporary world essentially through the actions of people on land, past and present. How those actions are captured visually becomes extremely important in looking for wisdom on how to intervene through the production of architecture and space in ethical and imaginative ways. I consider it as a moment of luck that I encountered Feni's work because his images are consistently capturing and noting visually the complexity of a contemporary urban society. Luck has transformed into the gift of continued opportunities in working with Feni on more research projects, where we are together developing a conversation about South African cities. His visualisation of inequality, structural violence and his own imaginative response through photography is in itself a reflection on human creativity, despite the constraints by those in power.

A Drain on our Dignity is an remarkable series of images depicting fragments of life in Cape Town. The photographs that Feni takes visualise a landscape that is both familiar to me yet also speaks of a world that I am a complete stranger to. I think it is exactly this paradox – this tension between an embedded sense of knowing and a floating awareness of my own distance from that experience – that elicits a strong emotion when I look at these photographs. Feni's images depict the tension of the insider view/outsider reflection very well. Rather than attempting to resolve the tension, it simply works to highlight his own sense of being part of the neighbourhoods that he photographs as well as embracing the distance that is created with the camera – of seeing the familiar in unfamiliar places. In a sense, I see his work as a kind of a map that is drawn from places and scenes that he sees along paths that he walks every day. His map is predominantly of Cape Town. His profession as a press photographer deepens the often simplified image of 'beautiful Cape Town', as he captures stories of people and their lives as they make use of the city in the ways in which they earn, relax, care for others and deal with crises.

Townships and informal settlements like Mfuleni, where he lives, feature prominently on his map along with Khayelitsha, Philippi and Airport Industria. But the inclusion of the double portrait of Ongezile Mkwehla and Siya Wandisa of Ntabankulu in the Eastern Cape shows Cape Town as many cities within a city, a microcosm of many cities in South Africa.

Cape Town's contemporary struggles around development inequalities and service delivery is rooted in the past legacies of racialised spatial planning. The city itself is a living museum of the past's entanglement of race, infrastructure and architecture: let's take a walk that begins at the top of Longmarket Street on the edges of Bo-Kaap. If we stand at the top of the hill, we look down at Green Point Stadium, a major architectural contribution built for the 2010 FIFA World Cup and a key reflection of Cape Town's global economic aspirations. The stadium is next to the Rockwell Apartments, a development constructed over an 18th-century burial ground for slaves, indigenous peoples of the Cape and other persons marginalised during and because of colonial occupation of South Africa. Further along Longmarket Street is the Castle of Good Hope, a structure built as a defence against attack on colonial rule and in a sense the first major public space of exclusion in Cape Town. Our walk can then pause at the site where the neighbourhood of District Six used to be and where large tracts of land now stand, empty as a monument to the violent forced removals of people from this area during apartheid. This short walking museum observes spatial violence in its multiple terms – violence on the body and violence against the collective body by looking at architectural notions of power, control, exhumation and urban spatial genocides in Cape Town's city centre. Beyond the city centre, away from the mountain and the sea, racialised neighbourhoods, which we commonly refer to as 'informal settlements', 'townships', 'locations' or 'the flats', grew out of these moments of control and occupation. Luyolo, Ndabeni, Langa, Khayamandi, Lwandle, some of Cape Town's oldest racialised settlements, were conceived not as spaces for dignified human networks and interaction, but singularly within the framework of labour to serve colonial, apartheid and neoliberal interests. But how have people lived, built networks of care and human interaction with creativity, dignity and imagination in a city such as Cape Town, rooted in this exclusionary past?

It is through his camera lens that Feni places people's experiences, their joys and struggles within close proximity to one another. The main narrative in Feni's images is the lack of infrastructure to support the complexities and labour of everyday life – washing clothes, earning a living and caring for children. I once asked him what compelled him to tell this story, what was behind documenting how people go about their business in such precarious conditions. He said he was dissatisfied with the way in which the neighbourhoods that he knew well and struggles that he was familiar with were being depicted in the main stream media. People, in his opinion, were being portrayed merely in terms of their anger, frustration and powerlessness at the lack of care given to the built environment around them by those in the power to implement change.

'Every day we read about people's anger and frustration but we don't get to see the other side. For me it was important to focus on what these people do to make life easy for themselves.' He wanted to show the conditions that lead to the frustration and anger, and the resilience of people to make a dignified life under difficult and unjust conditions. In the absence of basic municipal services such as refuse collection, storm-water control, sewage systems, dignified and safe public spaces, and the provision of clean potable water, even a very ordinary chore like washing clothes becomes a refusal of the limitations set by modern infrastructural indifference. Washing clothes, in Feni's frame, becomes a form of resistance.

In this collection of Feni's, we see many portraits of children, men and women busy with various tasks: cleaning and collecting waste from the royal blue portable toilets which mark the neighbourhoods in particular ways; washing laundry from a wheelbarrow; throwing human waste at a car in protest; cooking food on the side of the road, feeding passers-by while earning a living; fighting fires that threaten to destroy a home; collecting water from a communal tap; playing soccer; doing backflips; commuting from home and back. People simply going about living their lives. The stories that Feni tells in these images are potent particularly if you link it within the wider discourse set by other prominent photographic studies such as Andrew Tshabangu's 2003 'Washing Clothes'.

In one image, Feni captures the ruthless rows of unpainted corrugated-iron dwellings, which line both sides of an unpaved alley. The alley is sloping towards the middle in order to collect rain water that would otherwise flood the newly constructed homes. However, as the image reveals, there is no place for the water to drain into once the heavy Cape Town winter rains begin. The seemingly endless repetitive nature of the architectural intervention of the homes echo the repetitive pattern of crisis: emergency construction, destruction by flooding or fire, inadequate reconstruction of settlements. Yet just as the cycles of modernity appear to be relentlessly repeated, so too are the determinations of Feni to render the world fully.

Perhaps the most moving element of the photographs in *A Drain on our Dignity* are the images of mothers and their young children. I once read somewhere that Feni grew up in an orphanage, having lost both parents at a very young age. Reading about his loss moved me, and later, as I looked at his photographs again, while also meditating about his childhood experience, it occurred to me that in his mission to document a fuller story of the vulnerability of township life, Feni was also in search of poetic depiction of a specific human relationship: that of the relationship between parent and child. We see Feni, for instance, observing a mother sitting with her child amidst the cold landscape of communal toilets in Klipheuwel. Or a young mother dressed in red and holding her new born baby on her way to a communal tap on the edge of a very dirty water channel in Masiphumelele. And what about the woman who, at a considerable distance from the photographer, is aware of him snapping the picture of her and her baby on her hip in front of her water-flooded home? Then there is the image of the mother holding her baby seemingly cowering at the distress also caused by habitual flooding in her area. Let's reflect also on the images of the women, the one with a school-aged child, the other with a baby's head appearing above a thick blanket on her back. In both cases, though, there is a wait for the police to arrive and move them out of Philippi to another place. In these depictions, we see something that is beyond the clichéd statement of 'walking in someone else's shoes'. It is a depiction of both a historical and contemporary portrait of the way Feni sees himself and the way he uses the camera as a tool for a continued search for himself.

Today, Feni's own access to sanitation is precarious. Growing up in an orphanage from the age of 18 months, he had access to safe, enclosed, fully serviced and clean toilets and bathing facilities. In exchange for adult independence and autonomy today, he has access only to the toilet of the main RDP house from whose compound he rents a Wendy house at the back of the property. He was recently able to buy a stand in another part of Mfuleni on which there is a toilet, which is connected to the City of Cape Town sewerage system. It is his immediate aim to build a house next to this toilet. Feni has achieved much with his growing archive of recorded episodes of everyday life. With his camera as the main instrument, he has artfully posed an antidote to the crude assessments of township life as depicted in mainstream media. He has, too, begun a subtle search for himself in the struggles of others with whom he identifies and boldly presented it for us to view and discuss. But Feni also has a desire to contribute, like others before him, towards a visual and contemporary account of the ongoing struggle for dignity in modern life as he told me in a conversation over a meal once:

> *I wanted to have some contribution to our history. If I can have this book it could be something that talks of the continuous struggle of the margins. Because since apartheid, these are the kinds of ramifications that the apartheid government has created so for me I look at the old-time photographers like Peter Magubane – they were looking at the current issue then, which was police brutality and segregation. So they were in the right space at the right time to be able to cover these events. So, for me, I wanted to maybe not to be like them but to continue the kind of campaign and [document] African history.*

– Ilze Wollf, Environmental Architect and
Co-Director of Wollf Architects

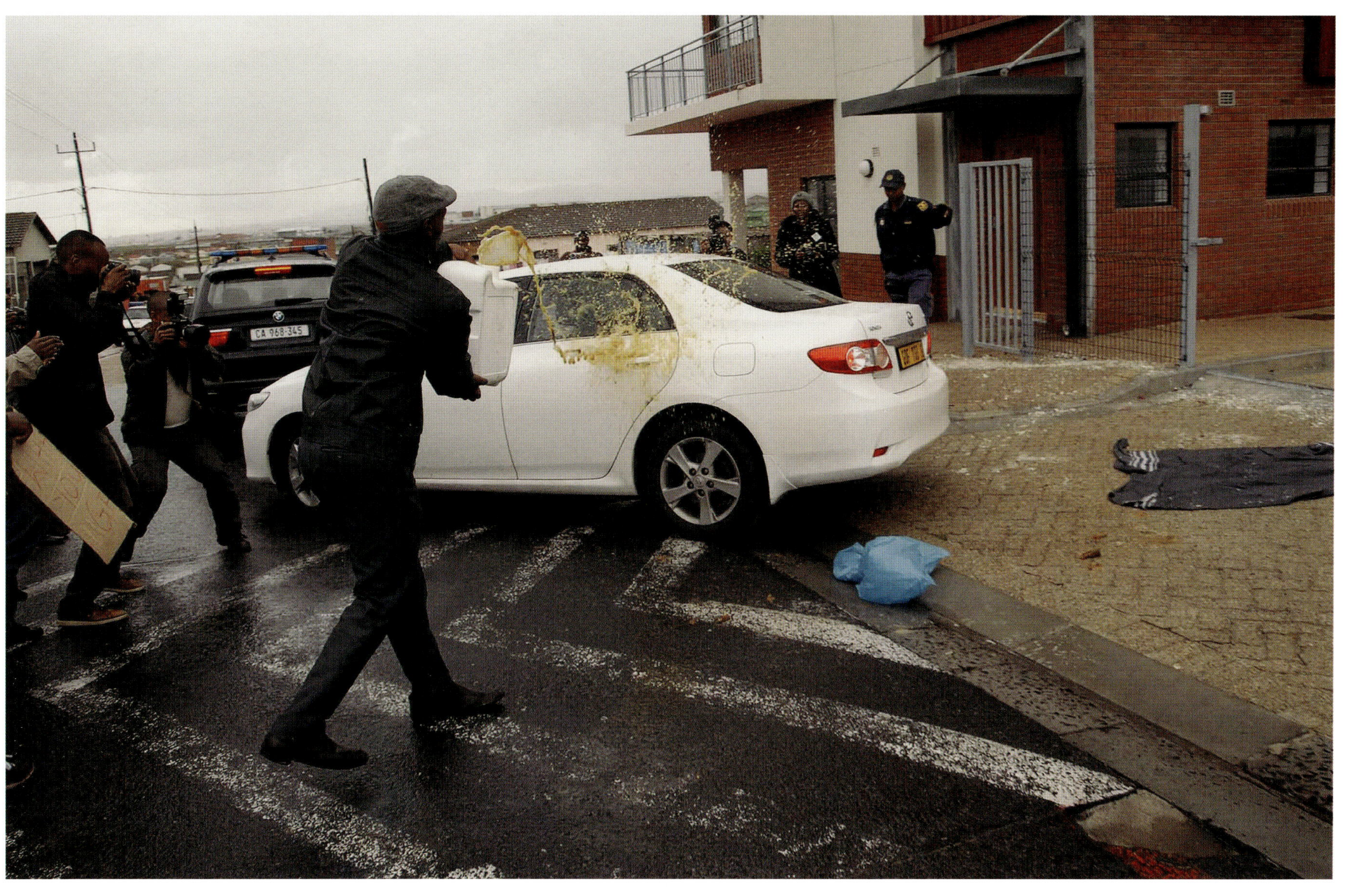

Human faeces being tossed at Premier Helen Zille's convoy after the Western Cape government held a meeting in a community hall to discuss service delivery. The meeting was disrupted by residents protesting poor service delivery.

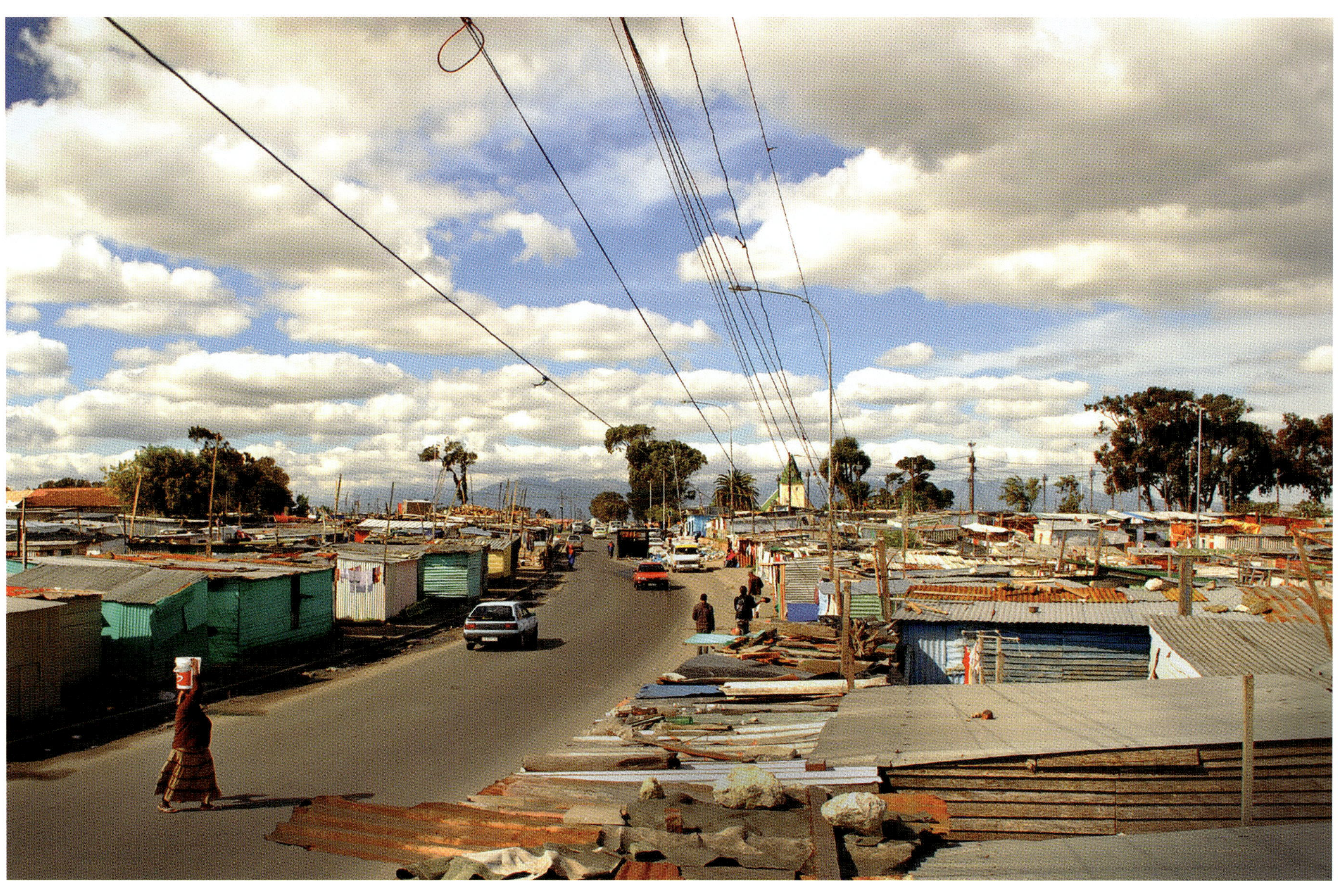

An old woman crossing a street in Philippi after
collecting water from a communal tap.

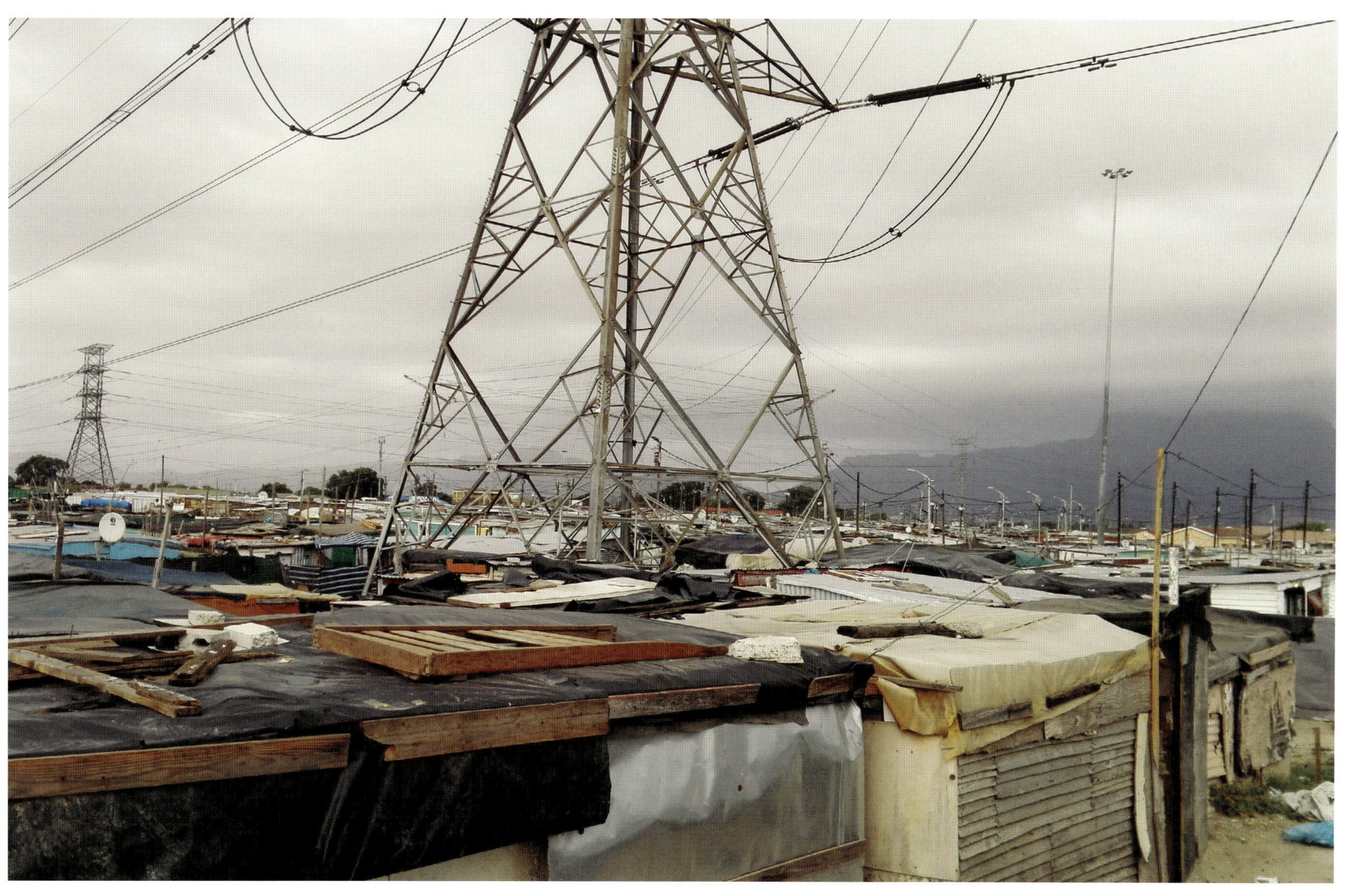

An electrical pole between a shack in Kwalanga in Joe Slovo township, where there have been a number of shack fires due to illegal electrification.

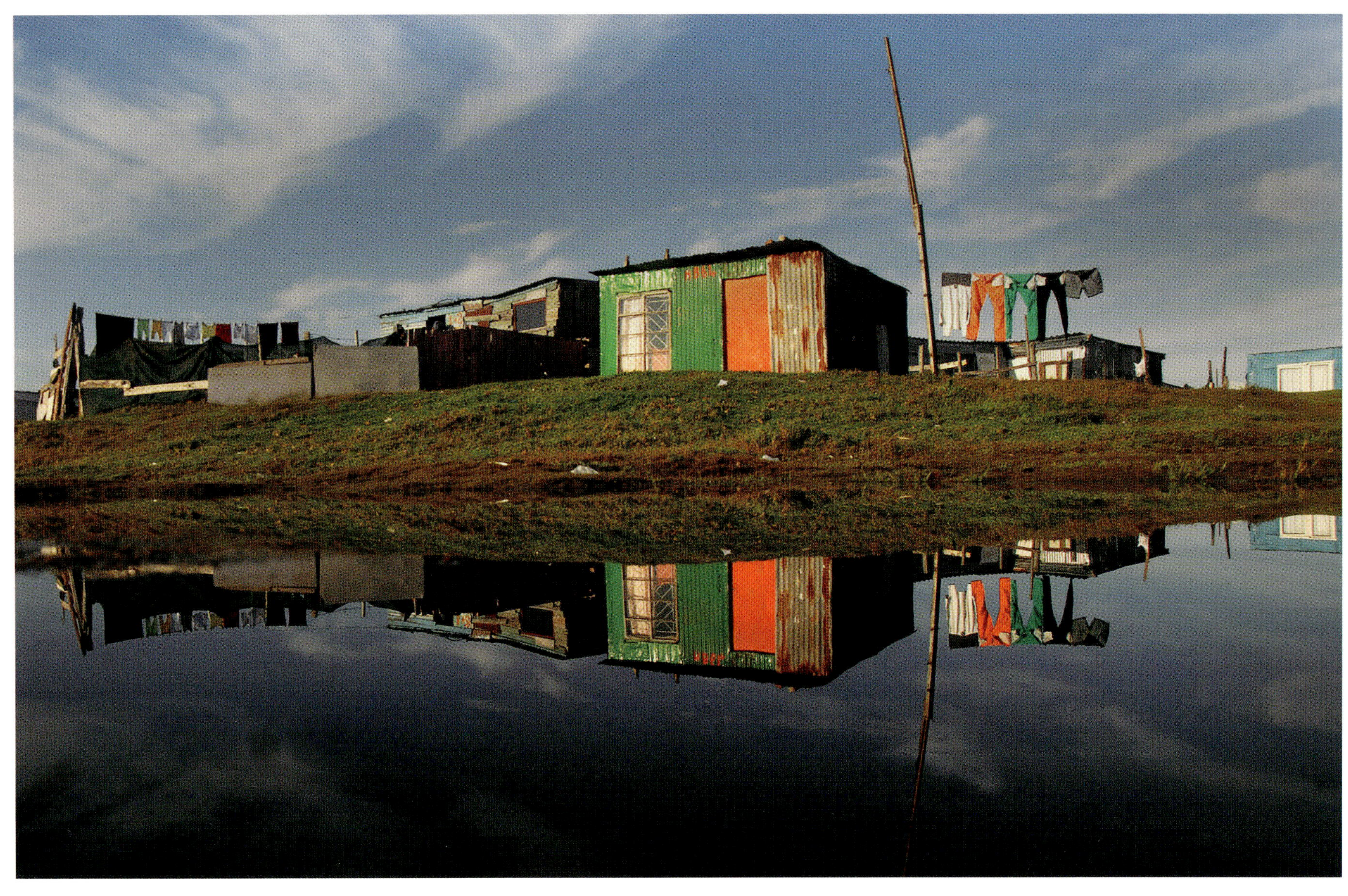

A reflection caught after some winter rain, Mfuleni.

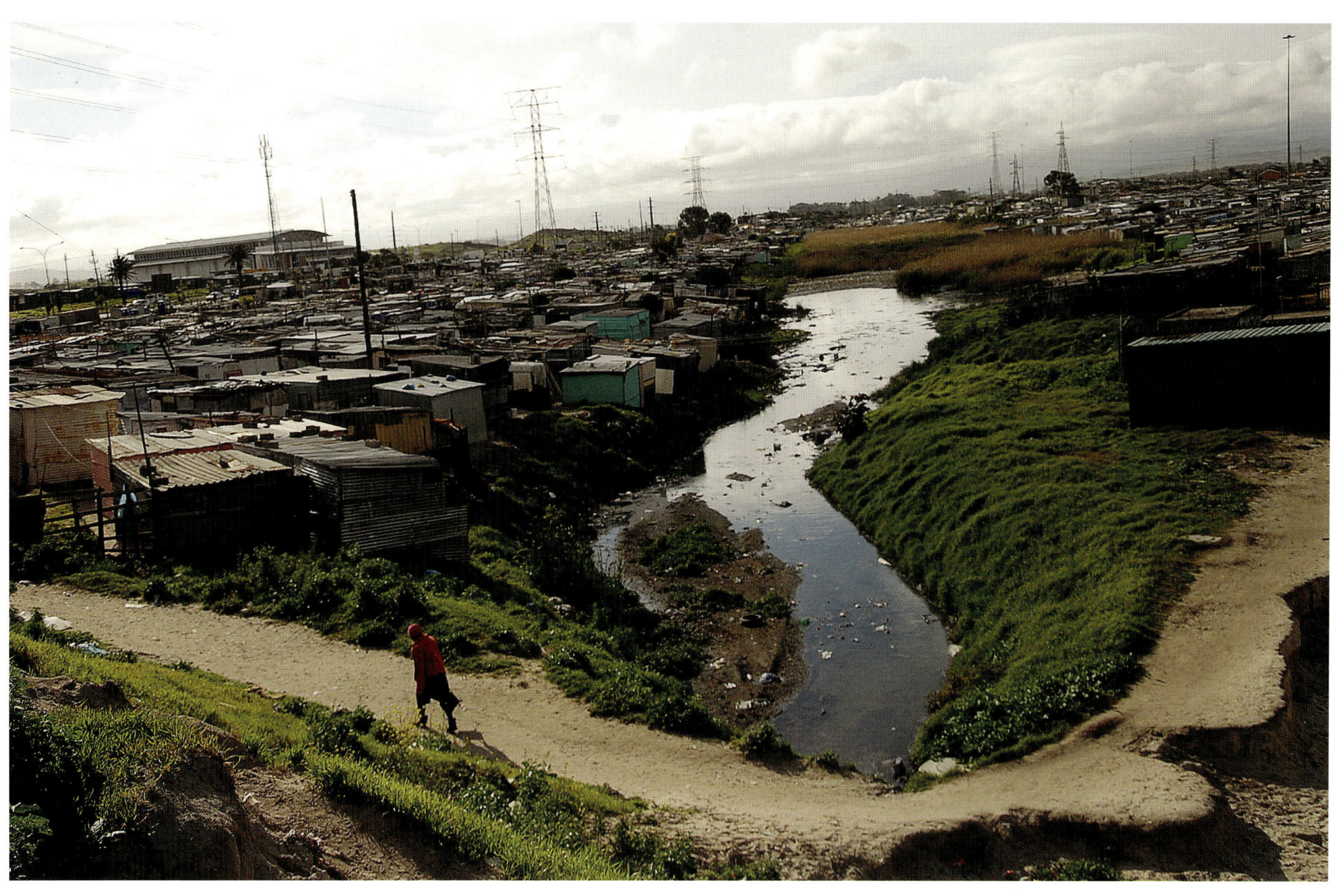

Undrinkable water: a canal at the entrance to Khayelitsha.

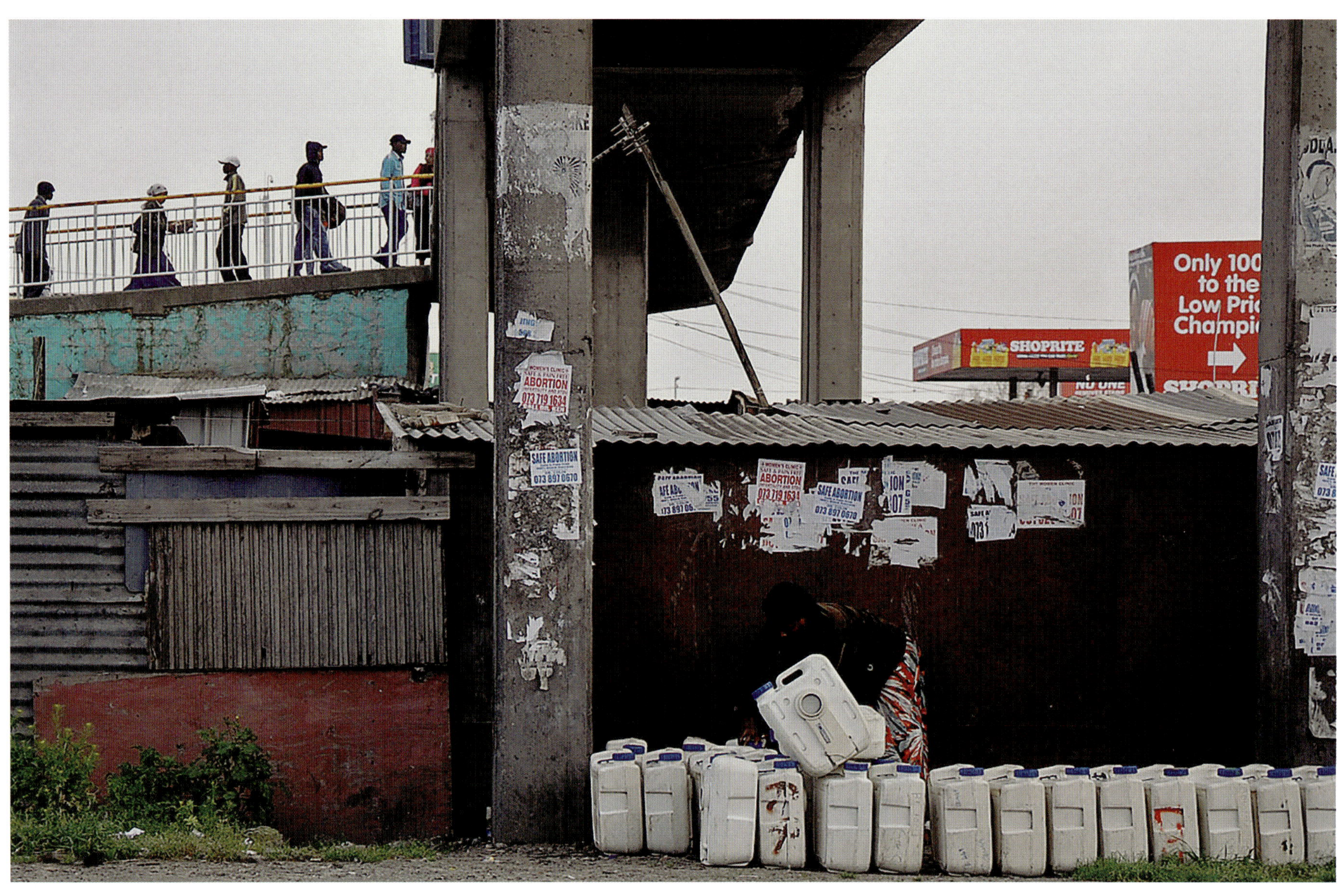

A woman putting the portable toilets in a designated area to be collected
and emptied at Airport Industrial, Site C, Khayelitsha.

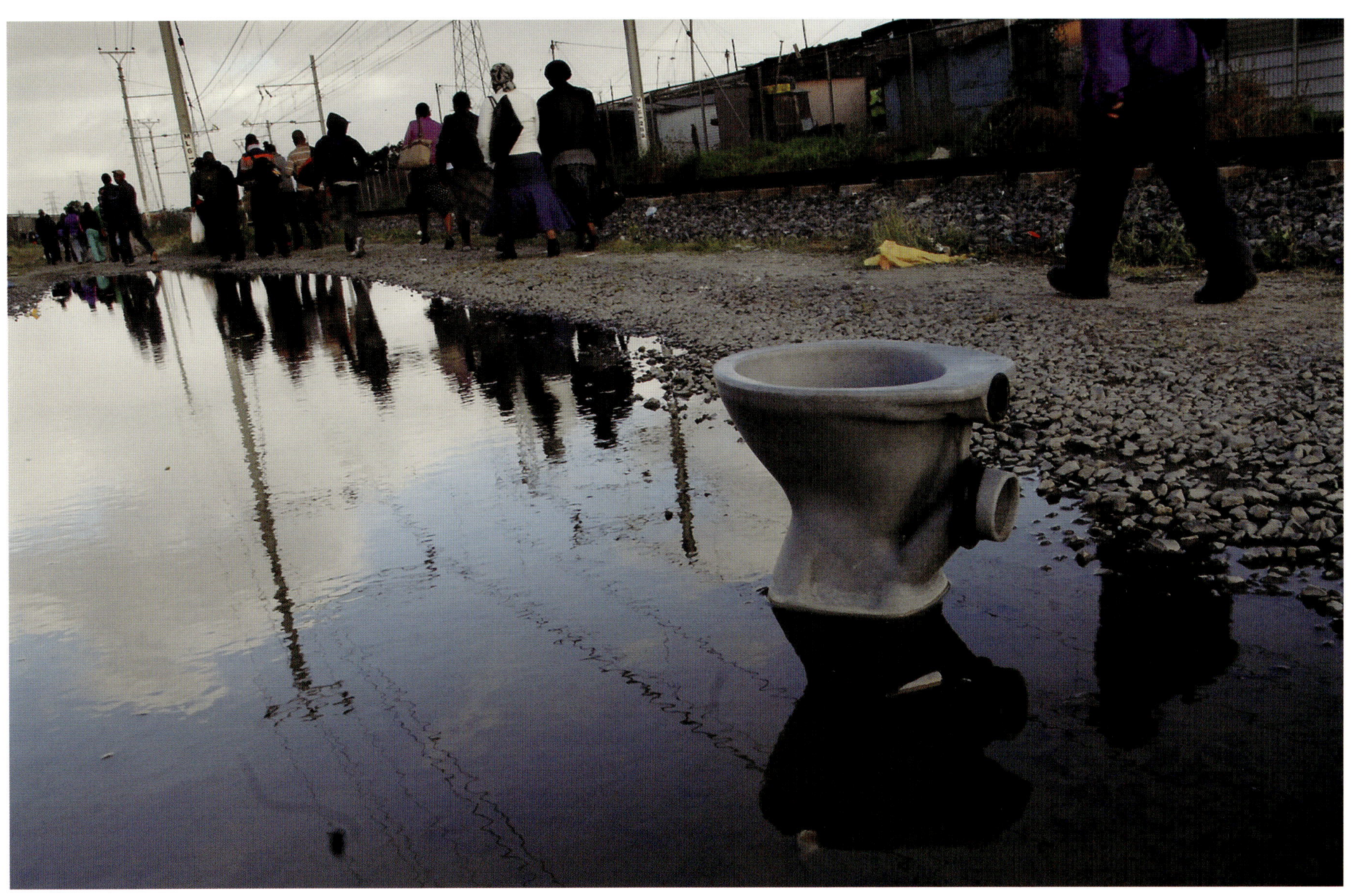

People passing an open toilet next to the
Nolungile train station, Site C, Khayelitsha.

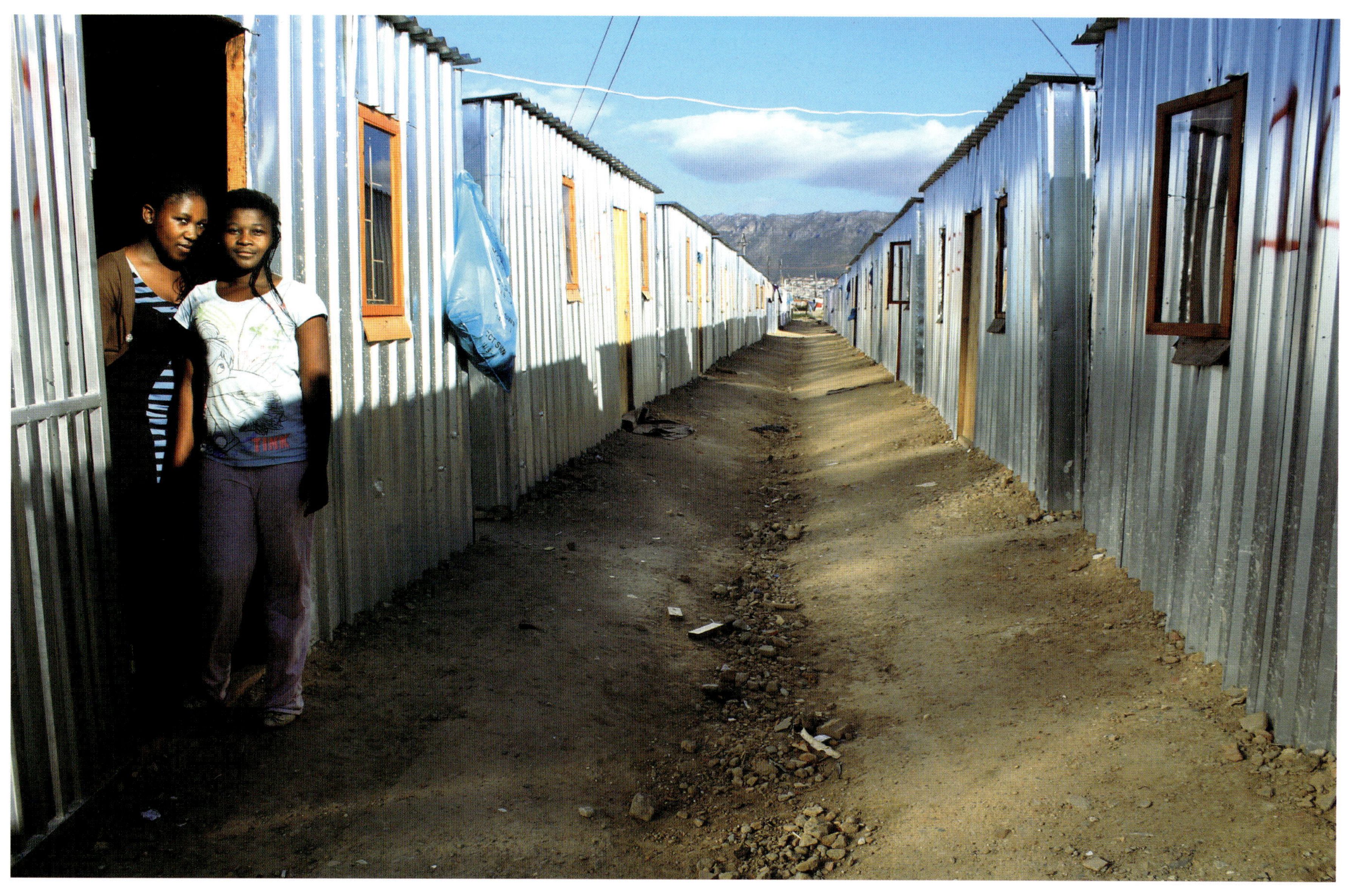

Two girls posing for a photo at a new temporary settlement that was built for the community after they were removed from privately owned land, which they had forcefully occupied.

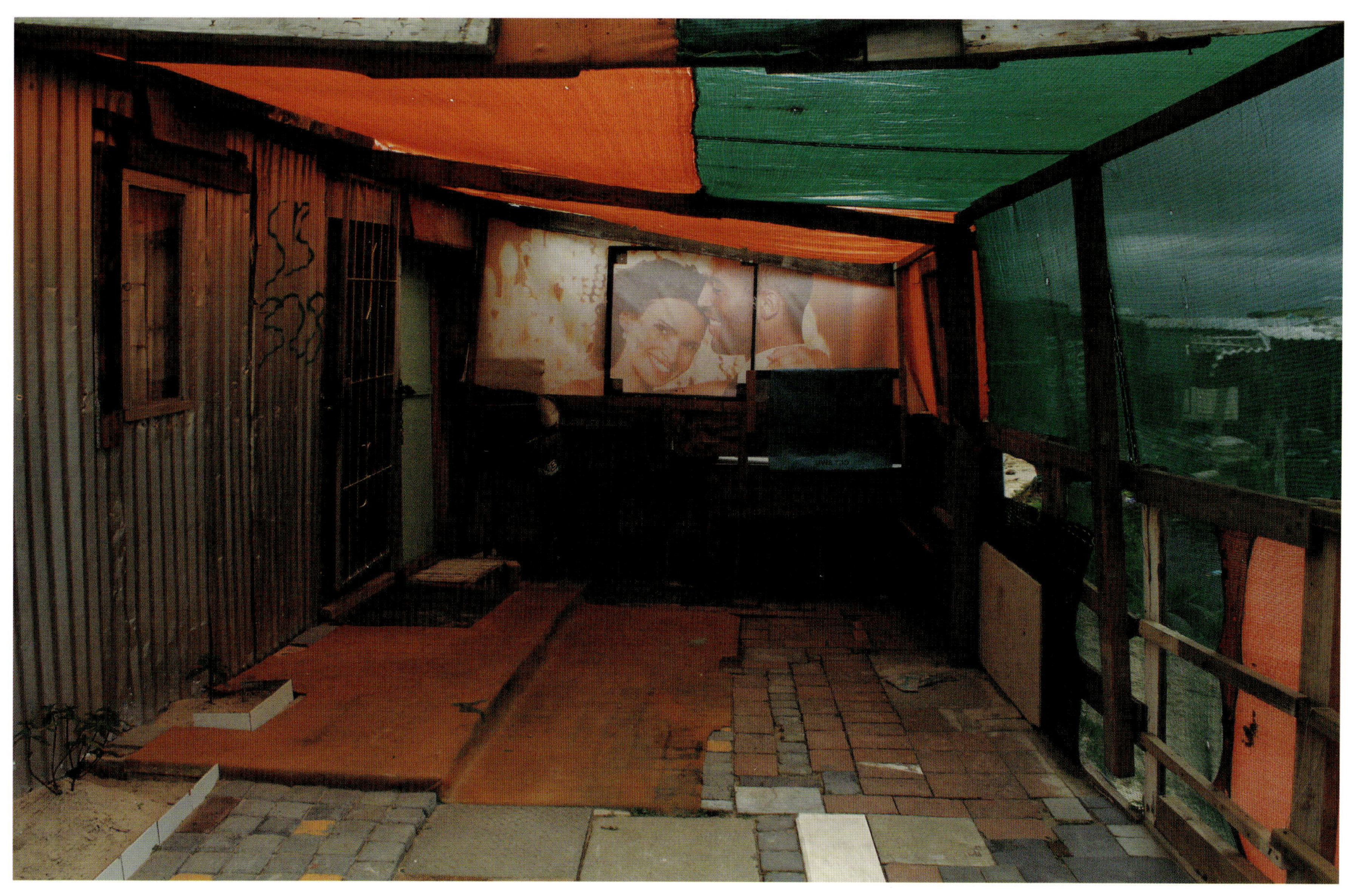

A home in Siqalo, a settlement that is almost always submerged
due to illegal dumping by demolition companies.

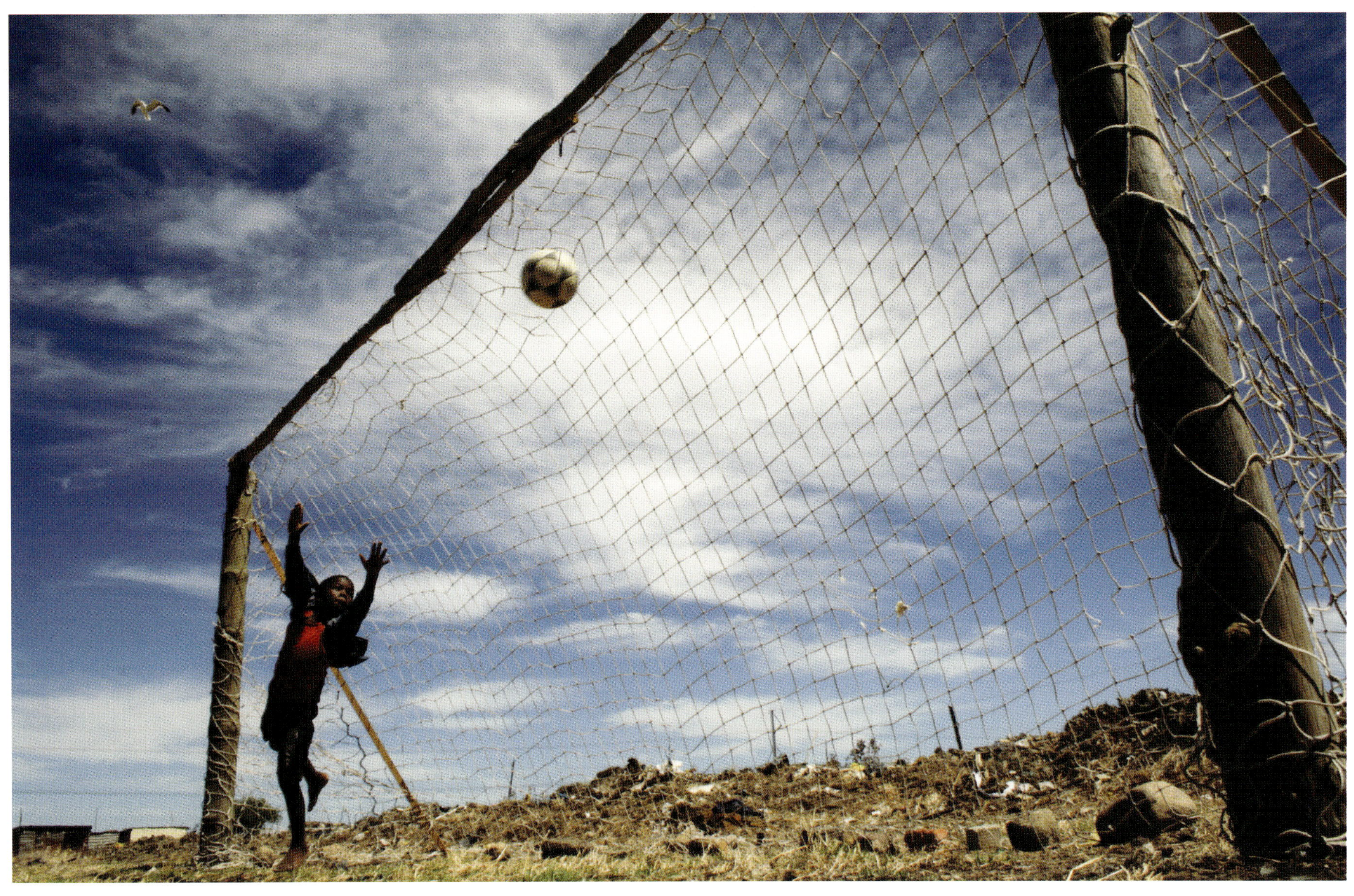

A young boy playing soccer on a rough pitch in Strand, Cape Town.

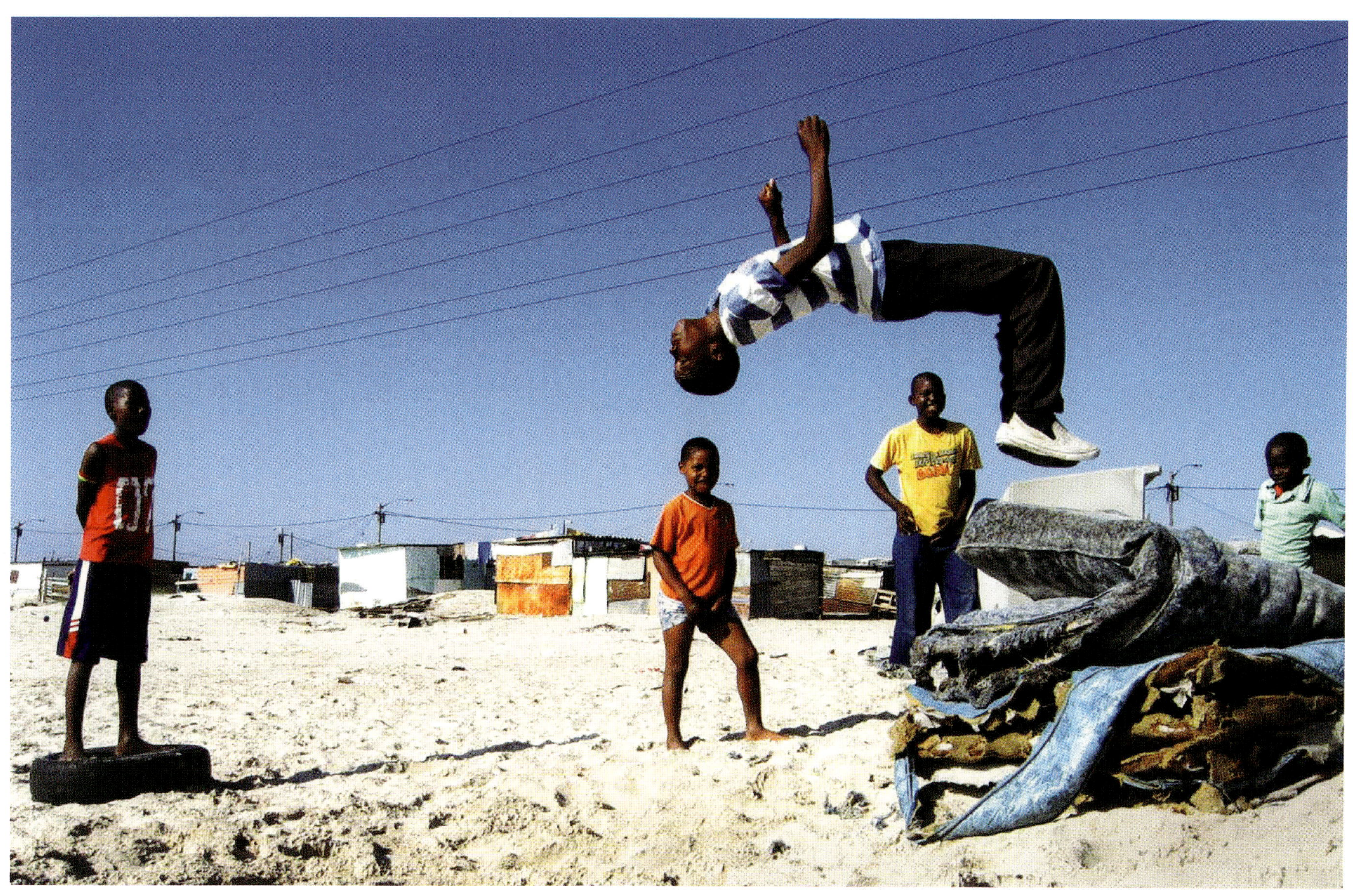

Boys doing back flips during the school holidays. Most townships and settlements in Cape Town don't have enough public recreational facilities. Children have to find ways to entertain themselves.

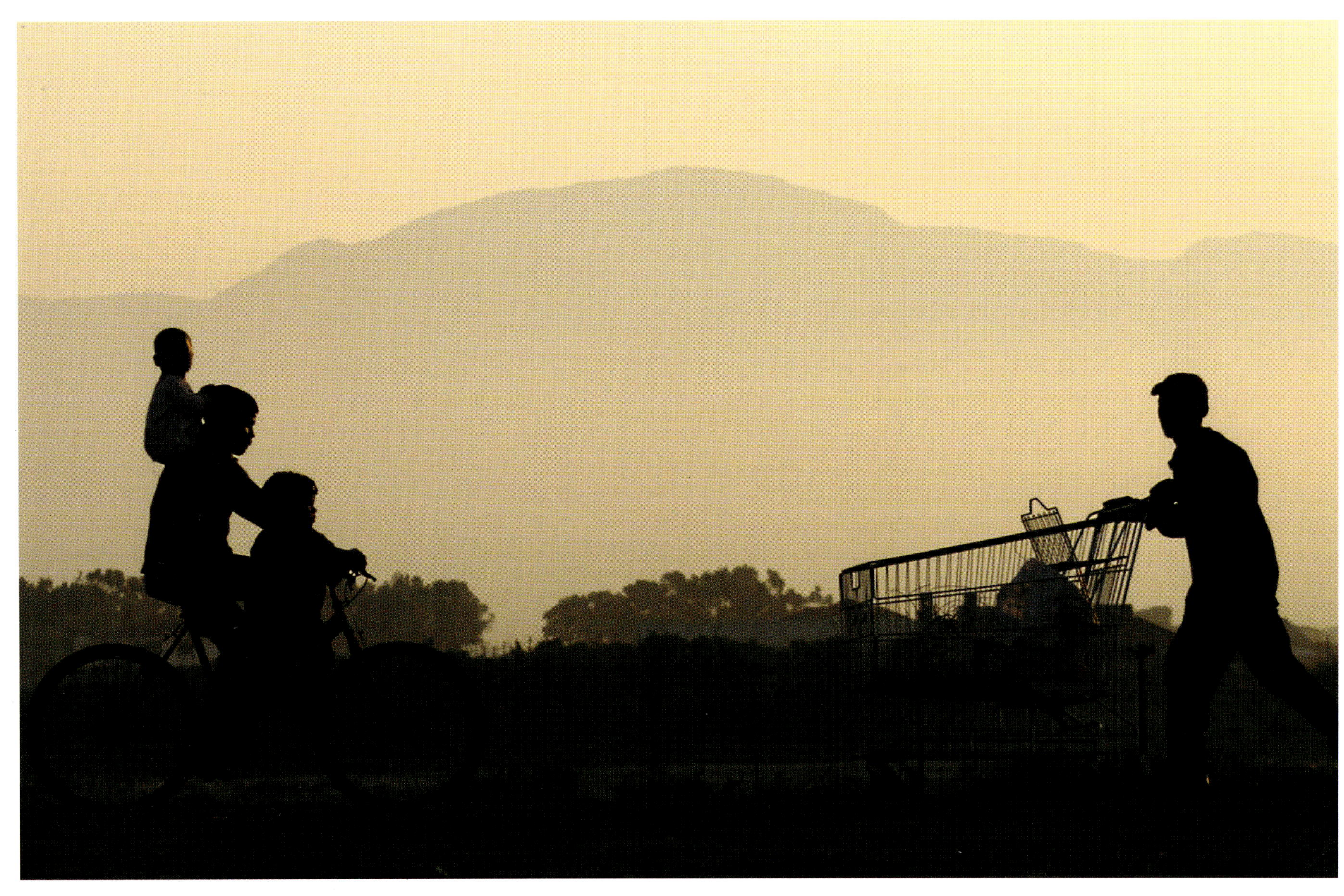

Informal vendors making their way back home, Mfuleni, Cape Town.

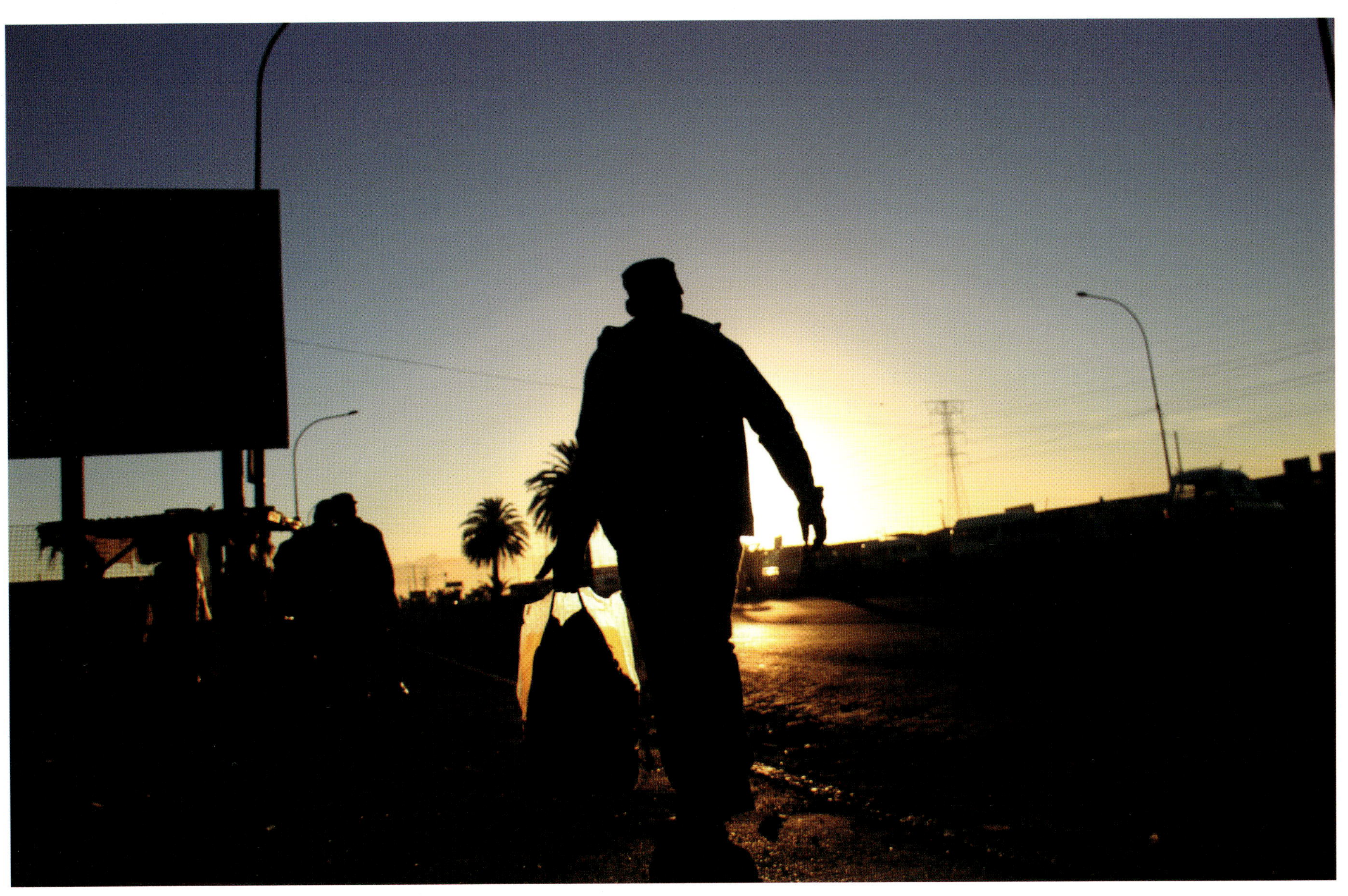

A man walking back from work – Jafta Masemola road to Site C, Khayelitsha. Most settlements are far from the city so that people leave home early in the morning and come back late at night from work.

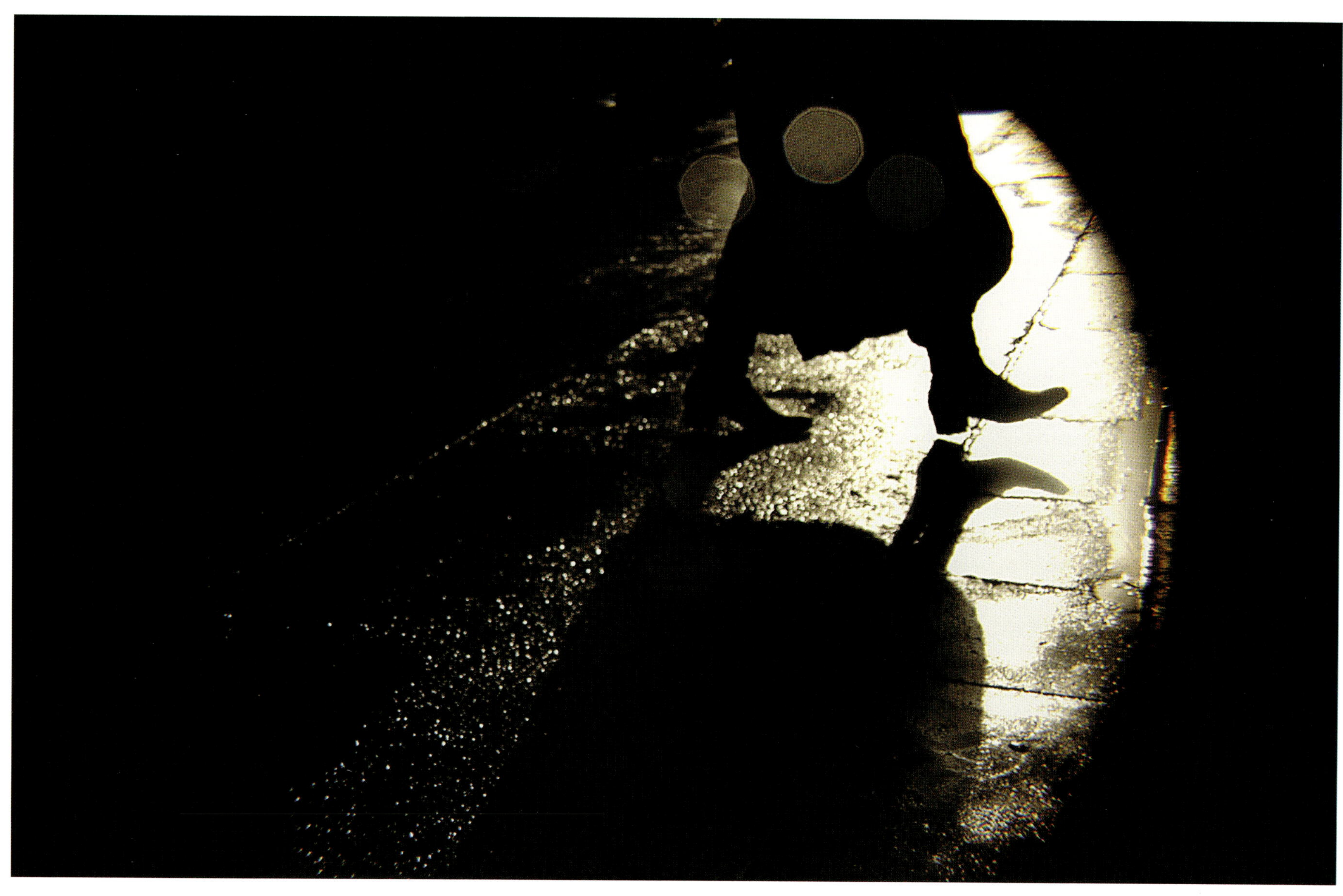

A woman walking to work before dawn.

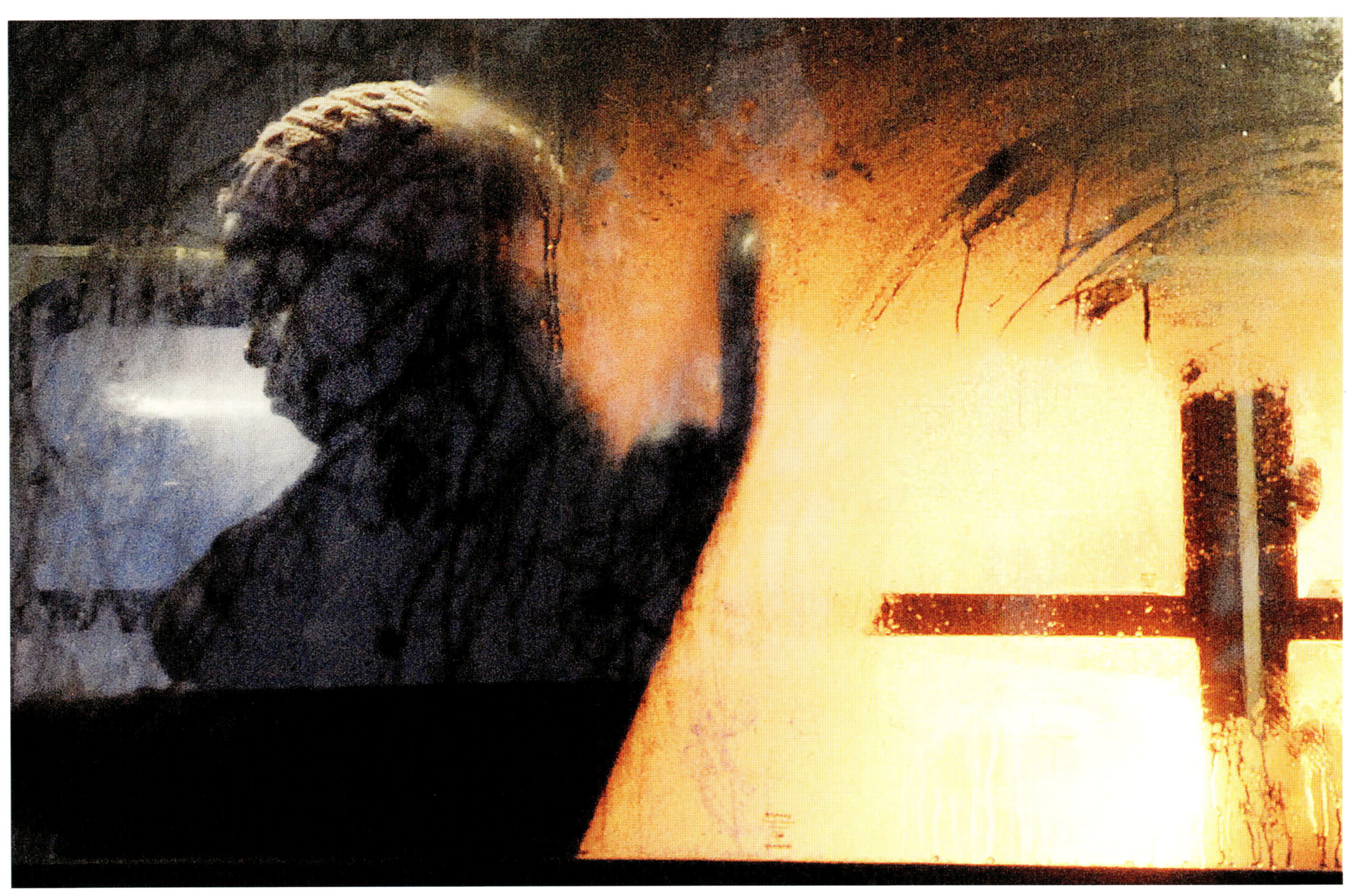

Most people use their commute to rest. A woman catching up
on some sleep inside a Golden Arrow bus, Mfuleni.

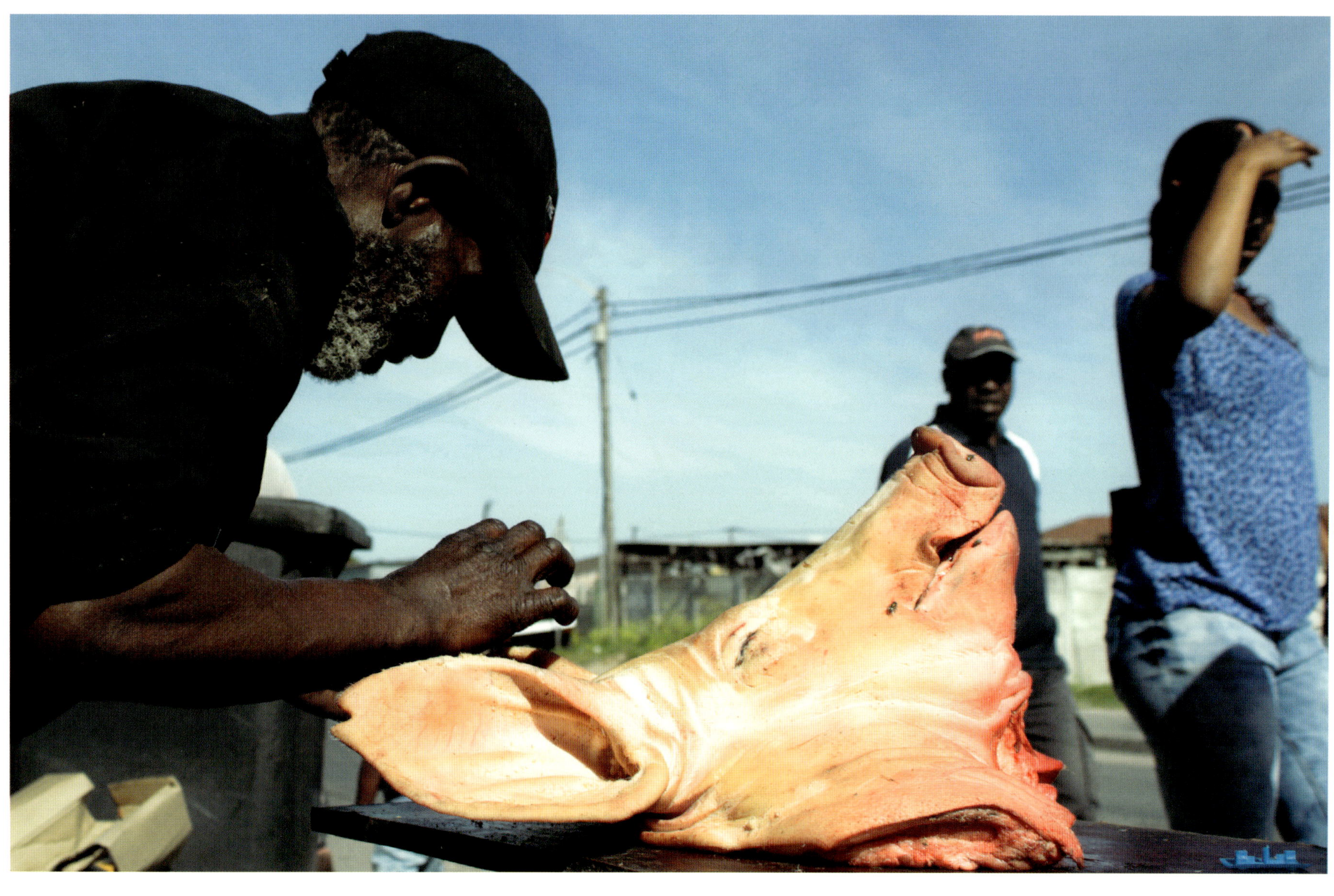

With high unemployment rates in the township, many people
turn to informal trading to make some money. A man
preparing pig's head to sell in the streets of Mfuleni.

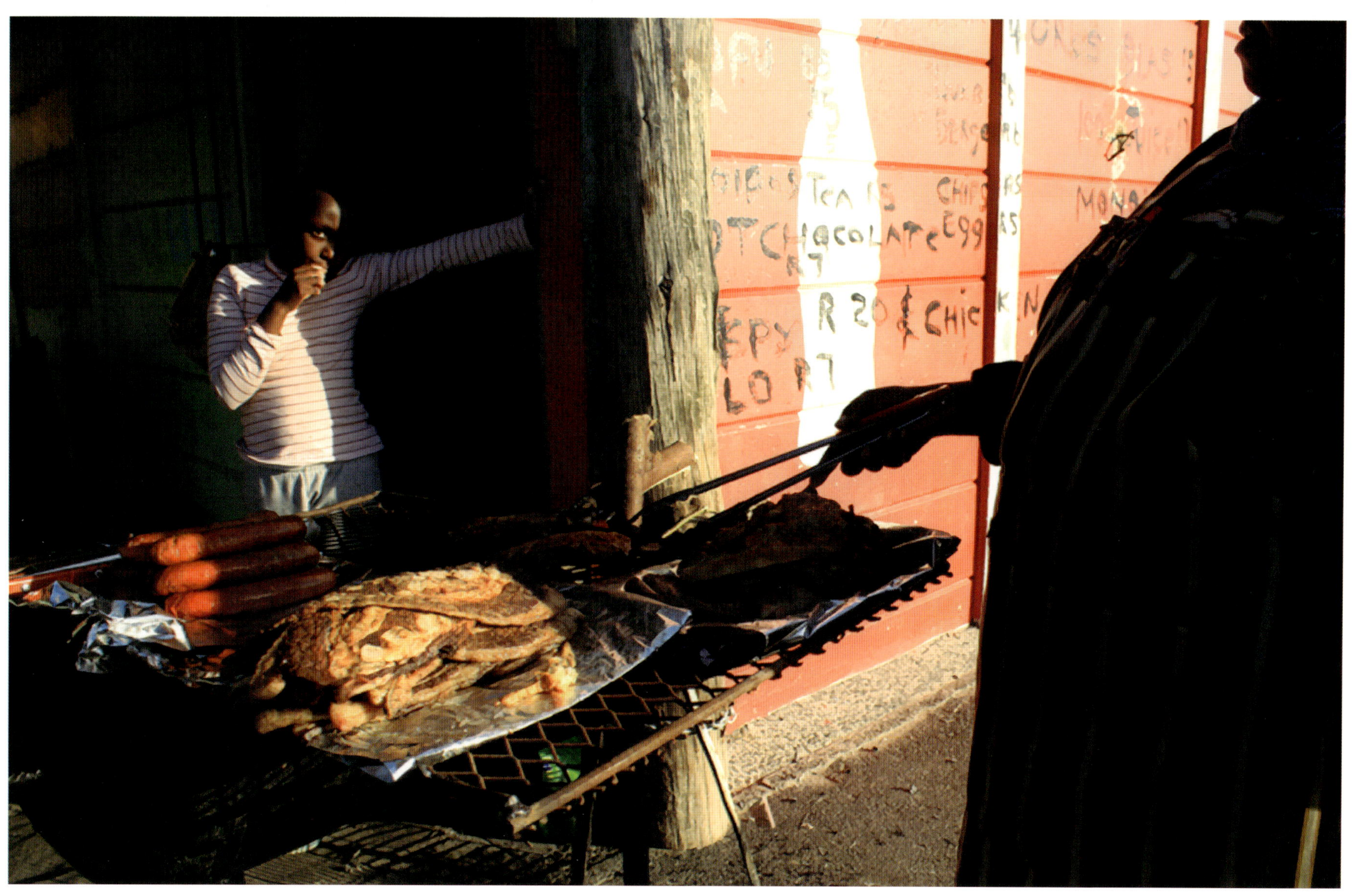

A mother and child selling meat from the side of the road, Mfuleni.

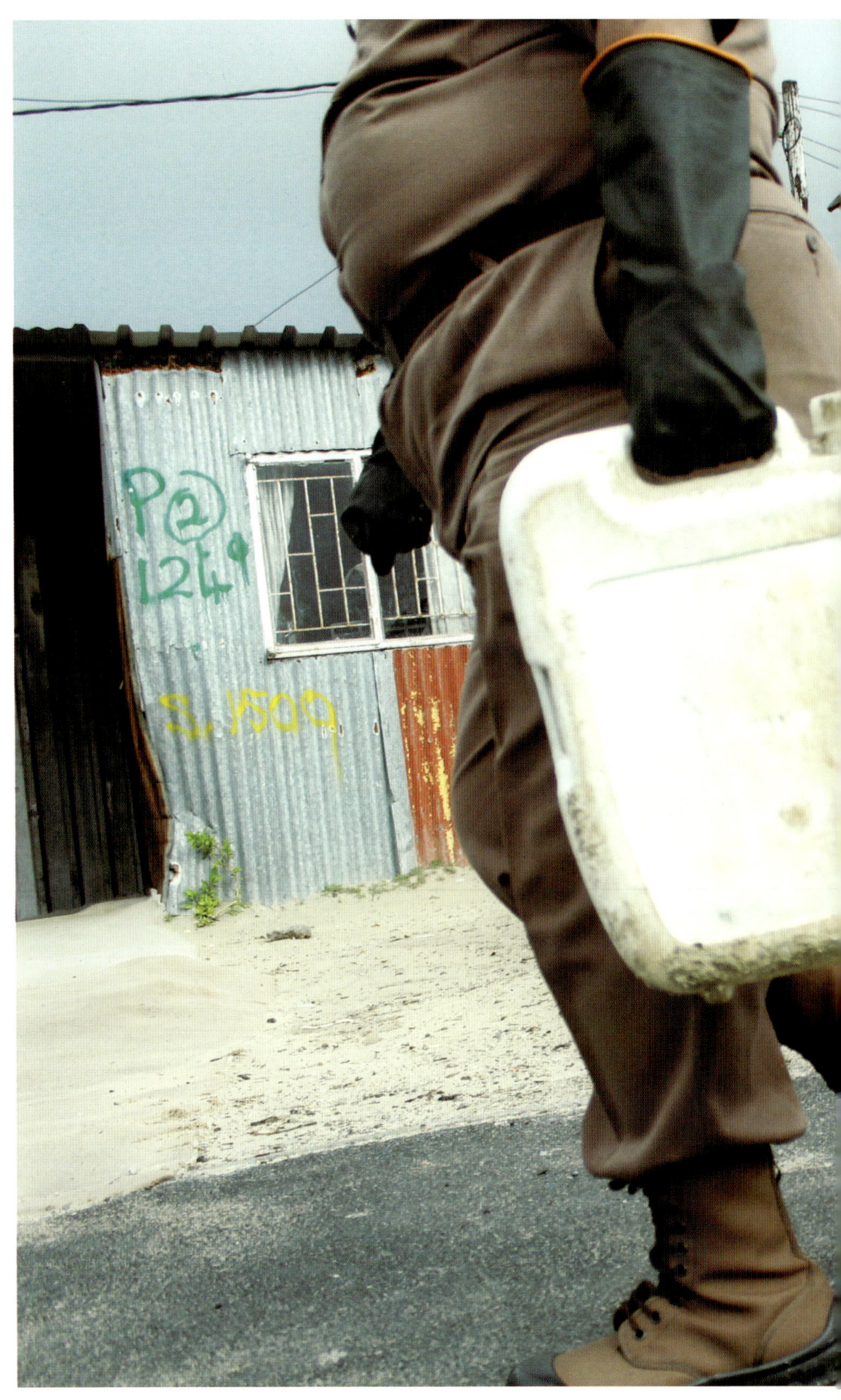

Correctional services workers collecting portable toilets in Khayelitsha.

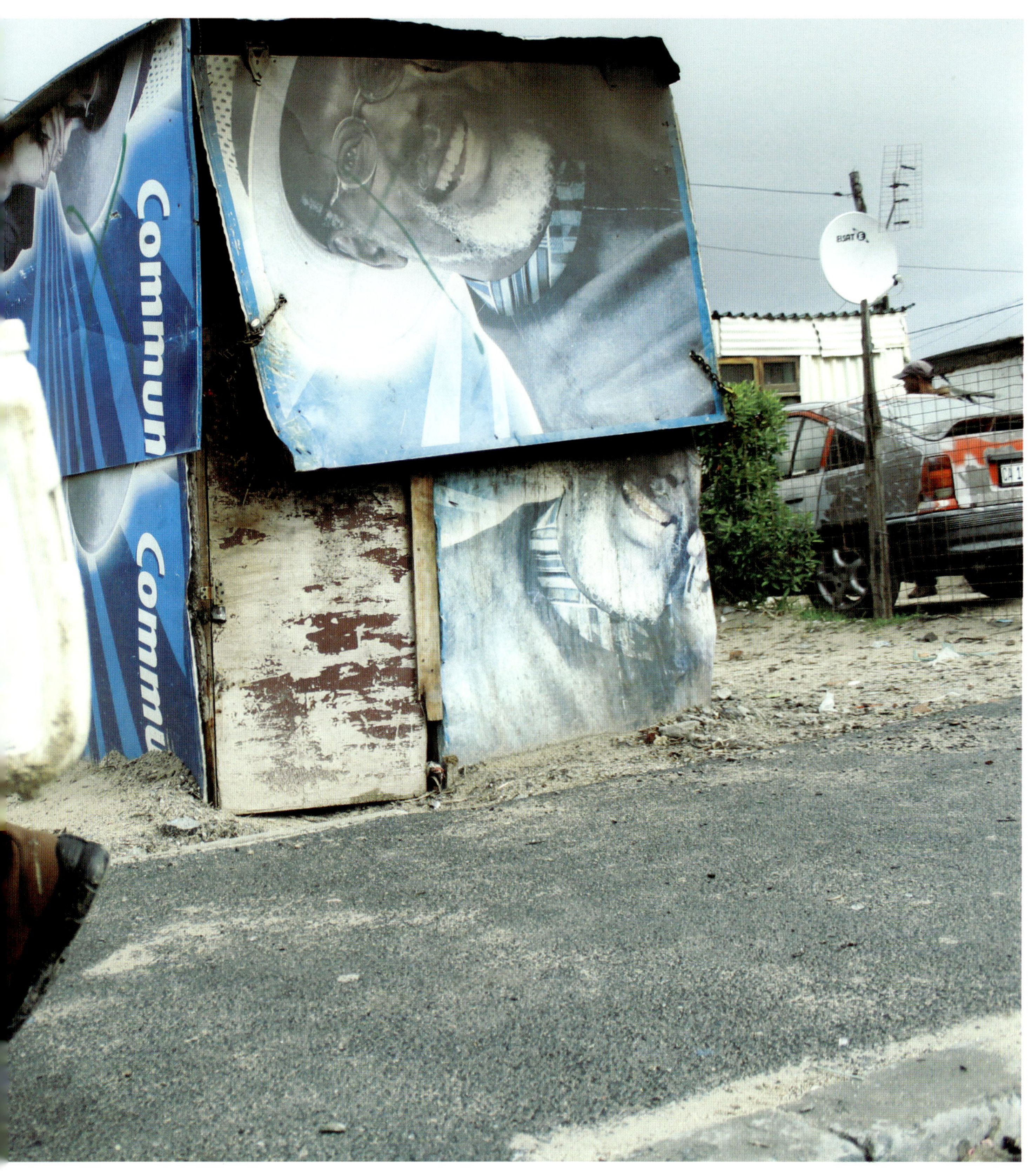

Commun
Commun

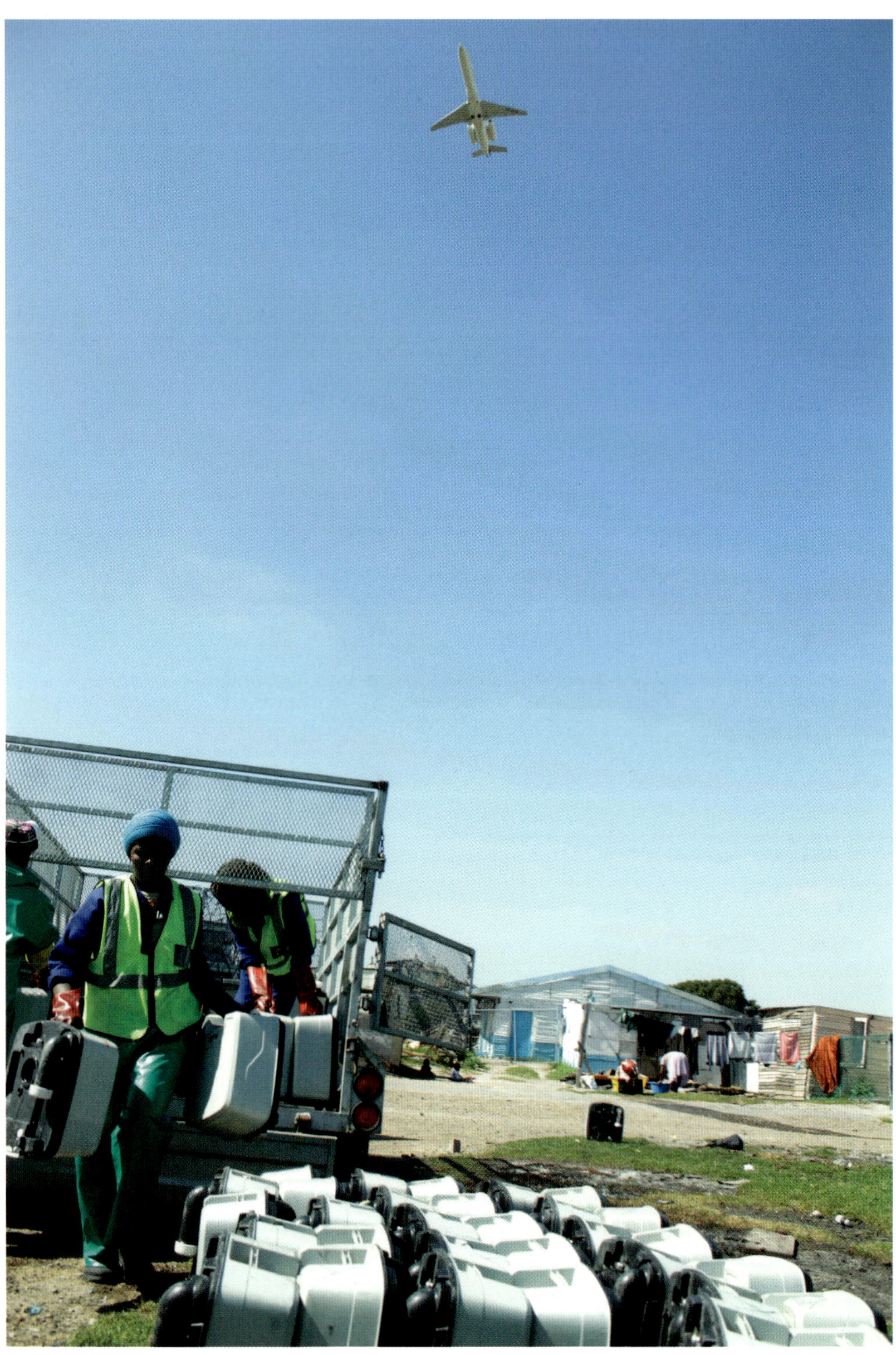

Contract workers collecting portable toilet waste containers in Freedom Farm, which is situated behind the Cape Town International Airport.

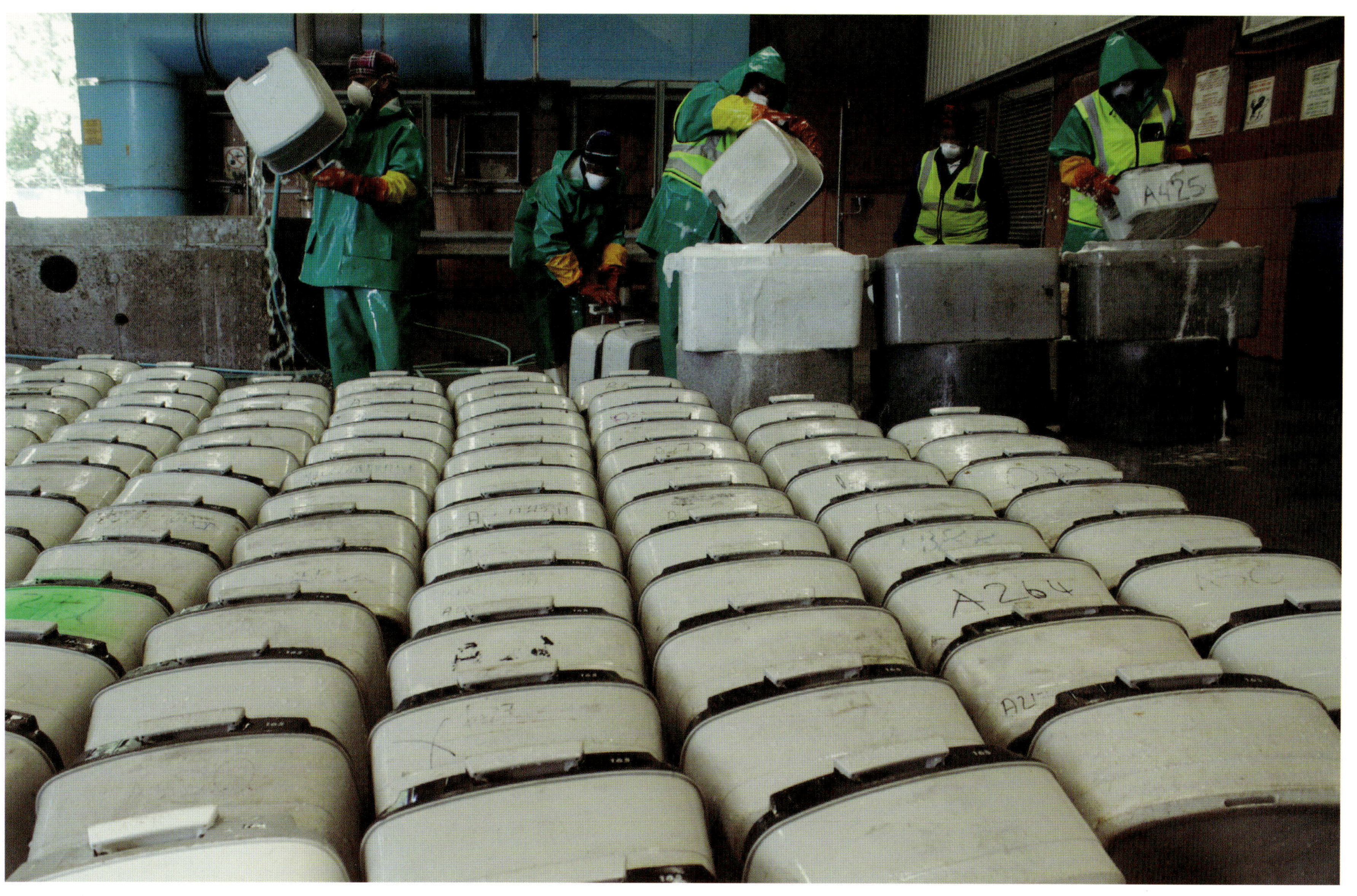

The portable toilet containers are taken to a big warehouse in Airport Industrial, where they are emptied and cleaned.

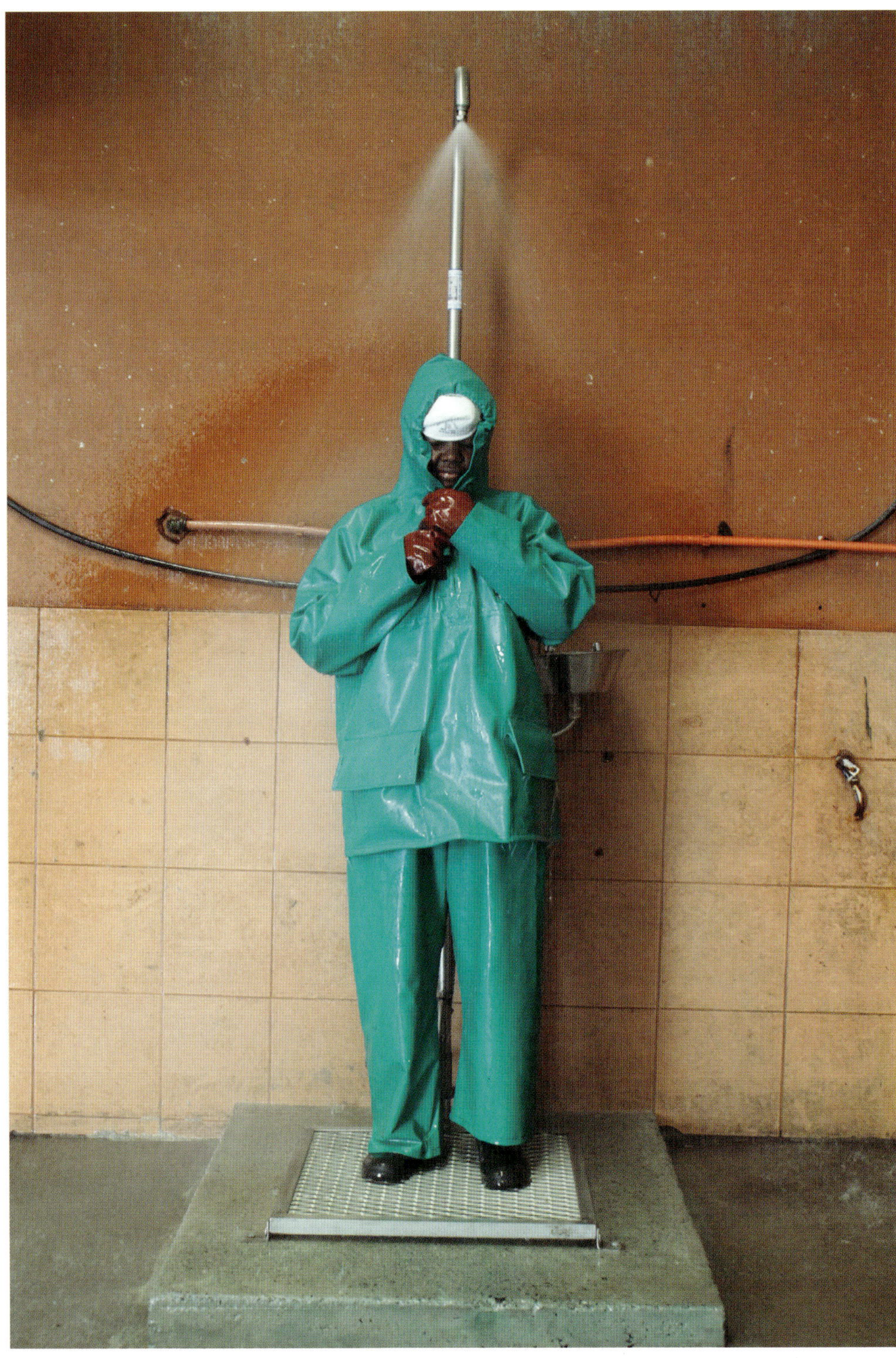

A man taking a shower after a long day spent emptying portable toilets, Airport Industrial.

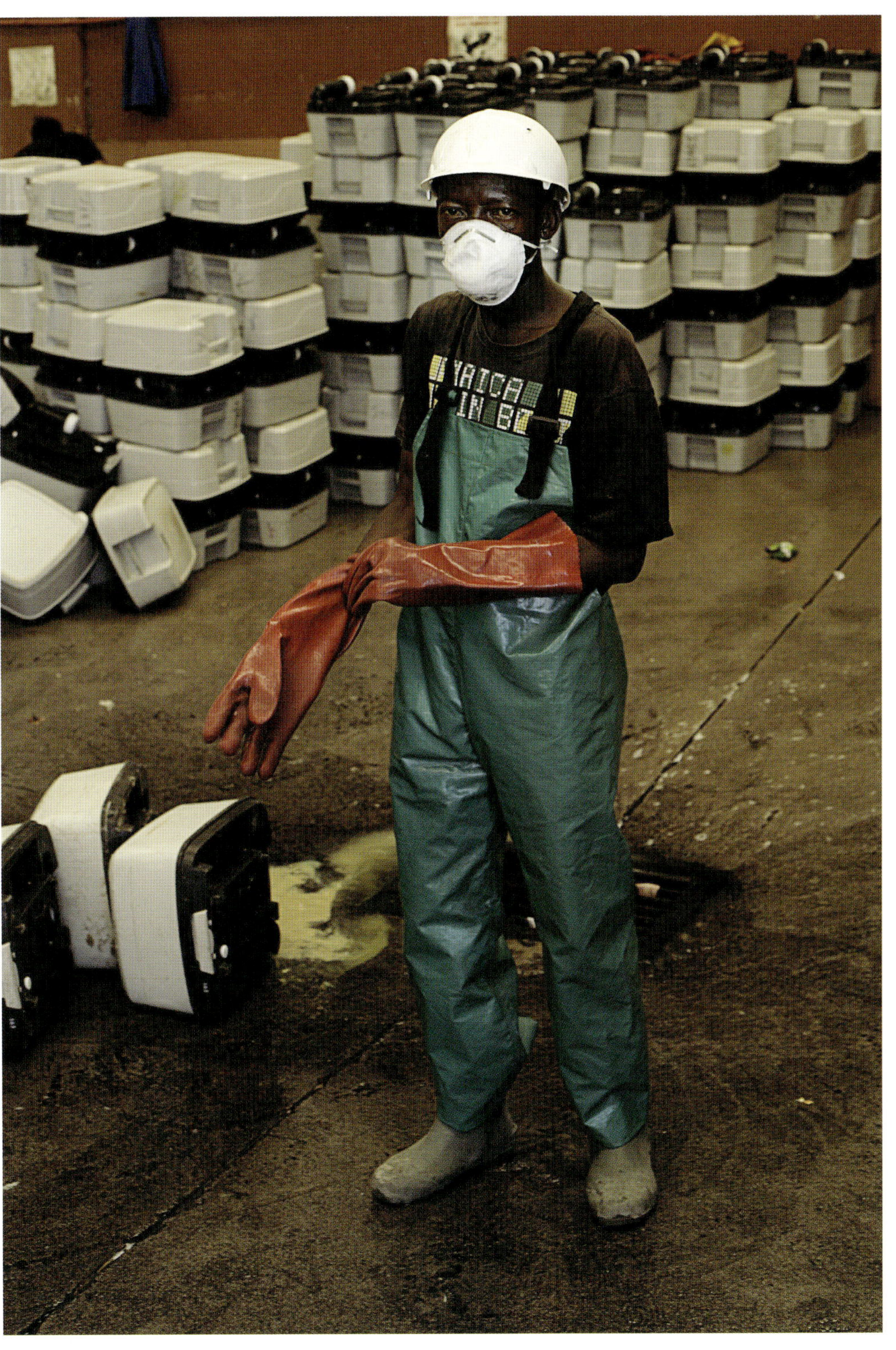

Putting on gloves before starting his work of emptying toilets, Airport Industrial.

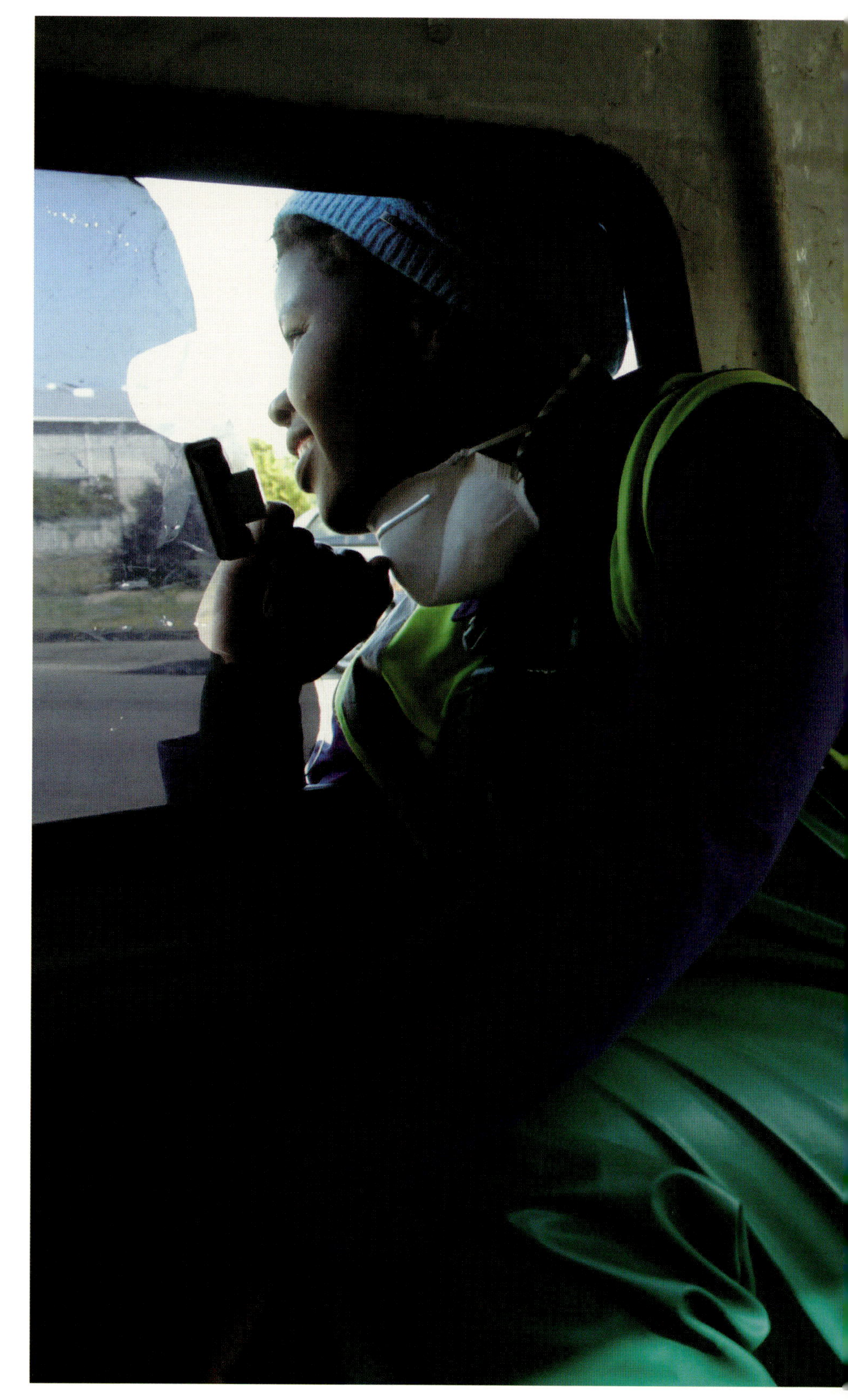

Contract workers taking portable toilet waste containers to Airport Industrial to be emptied. Some have to travel in the back of the bakkie with the waste containers.

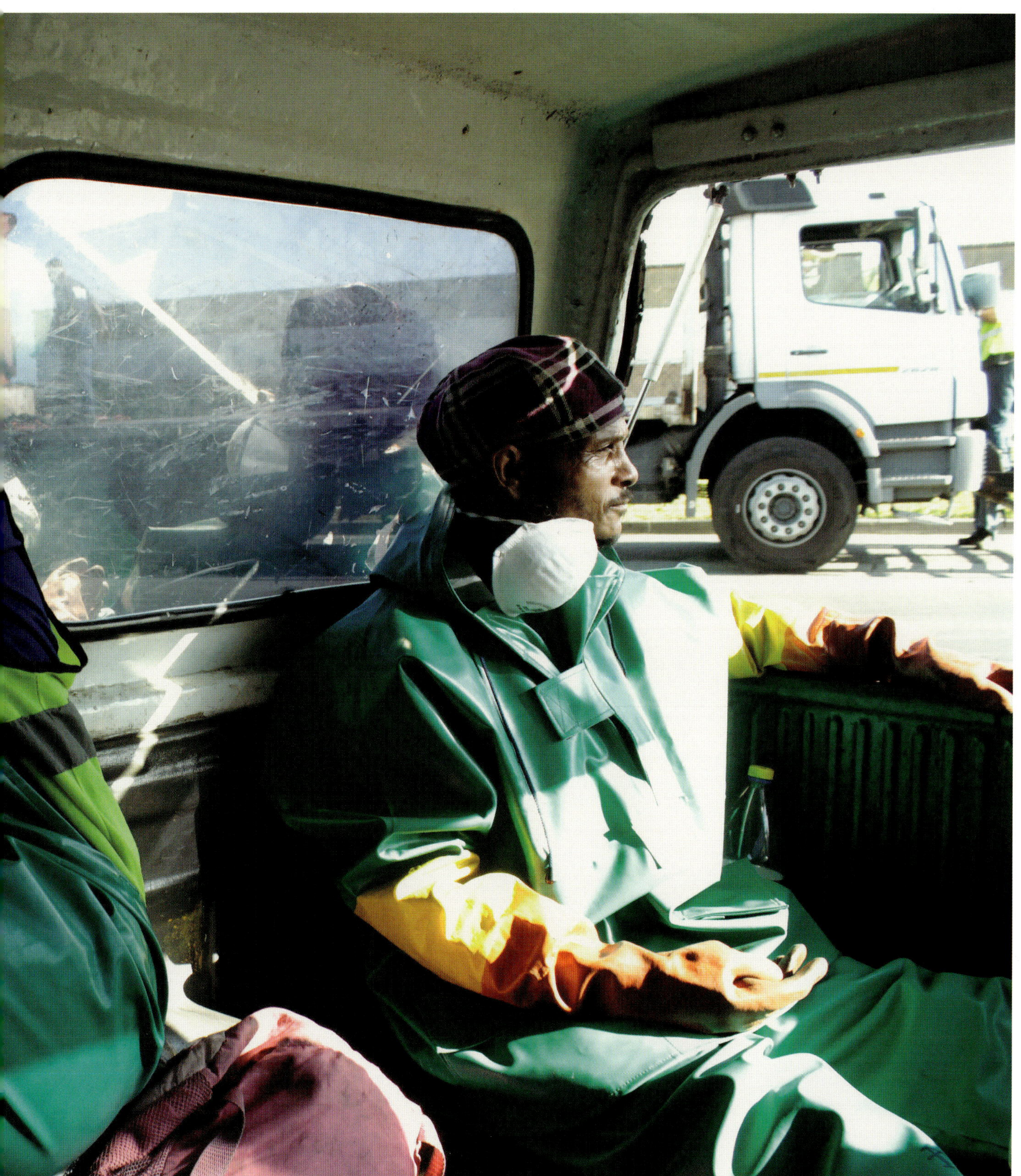

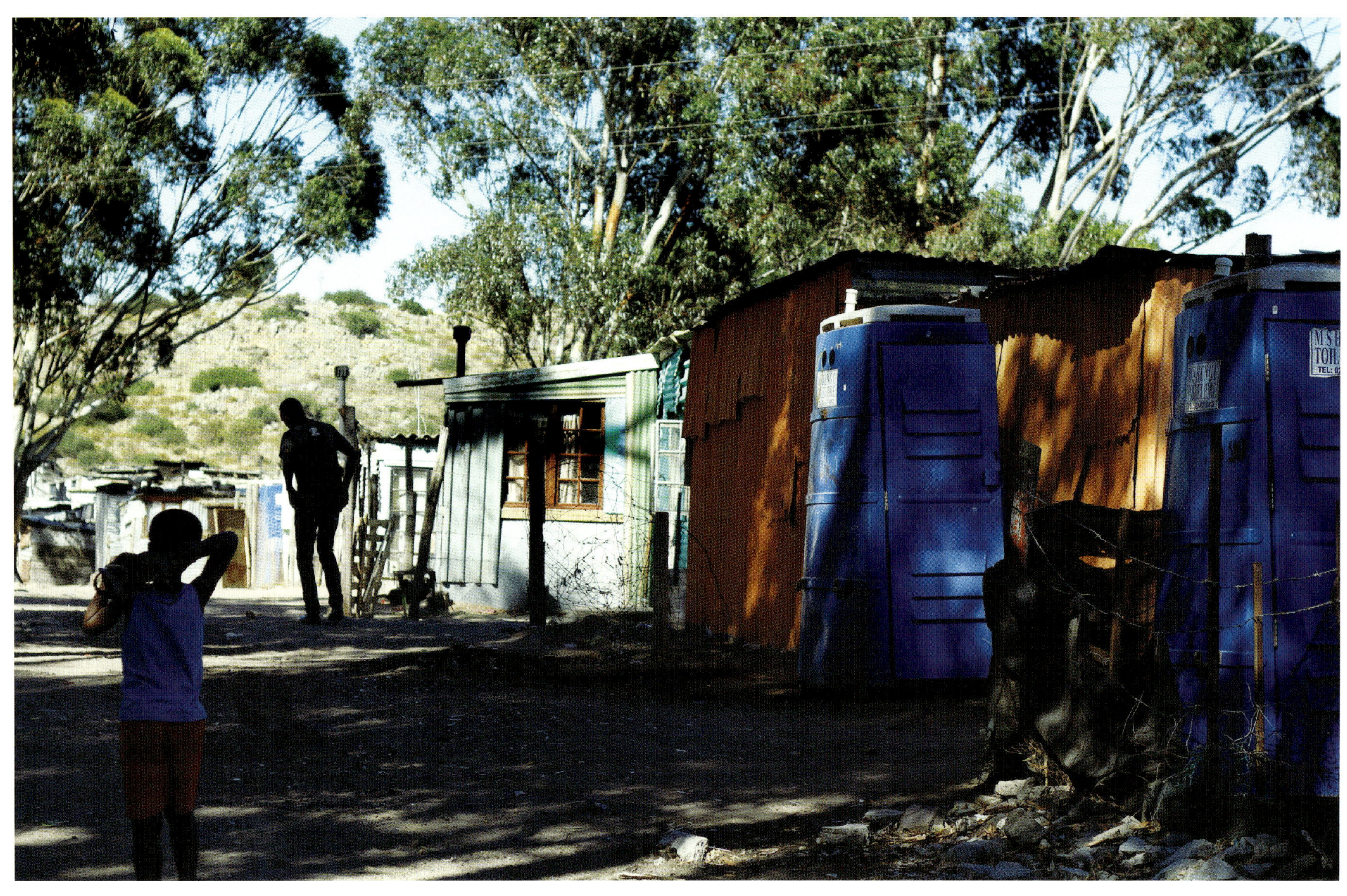

A child seen passing the communal toilet in Klipheuwel, a township outside
Durbanville, which is an affluent area famous for its vineyards.

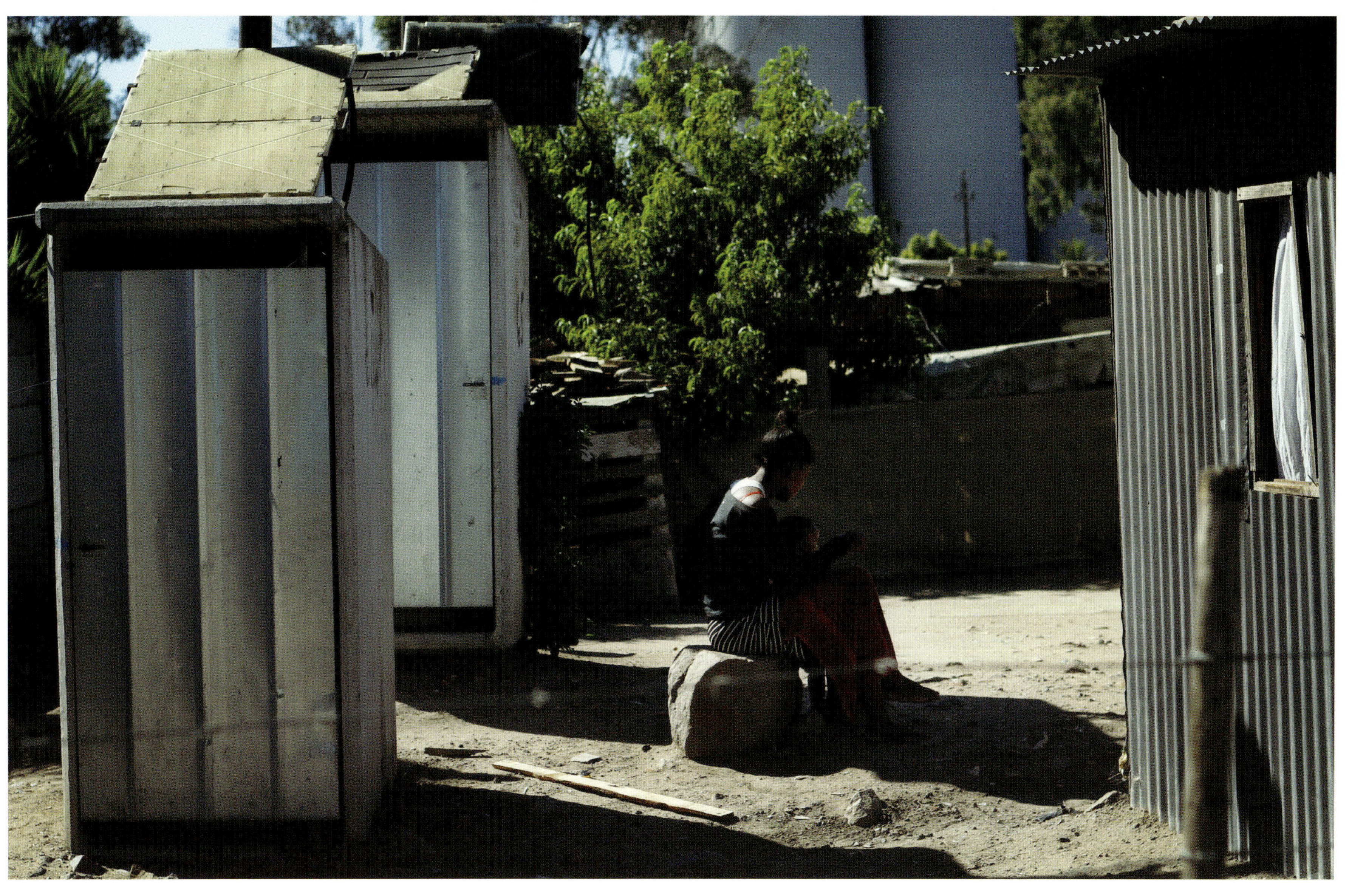

A mother and child resting between communal toilets, Durbanville, Cape Town.

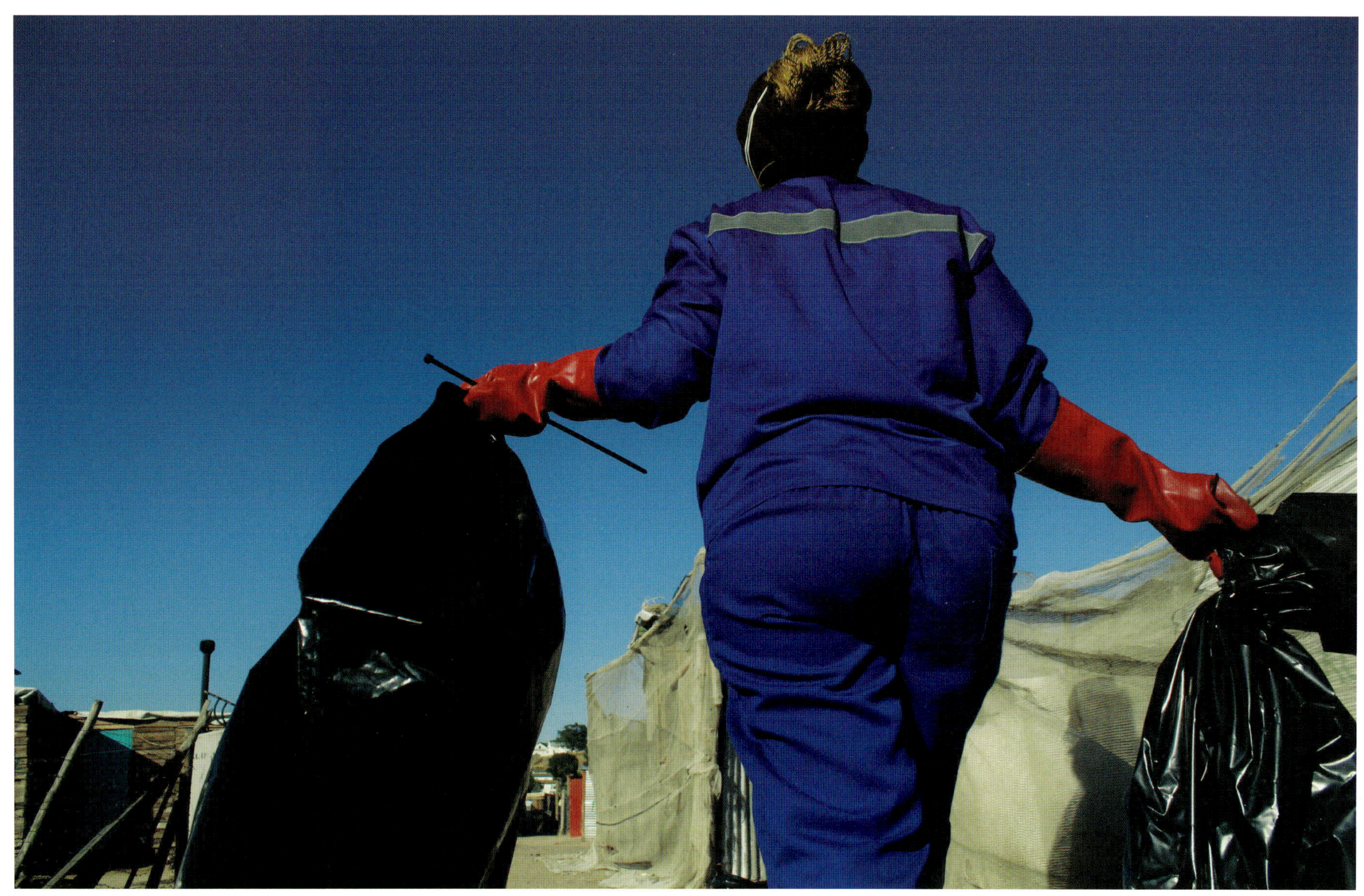

A contract worker collecting faeces in the black bags provided
by the City of Cape Town.

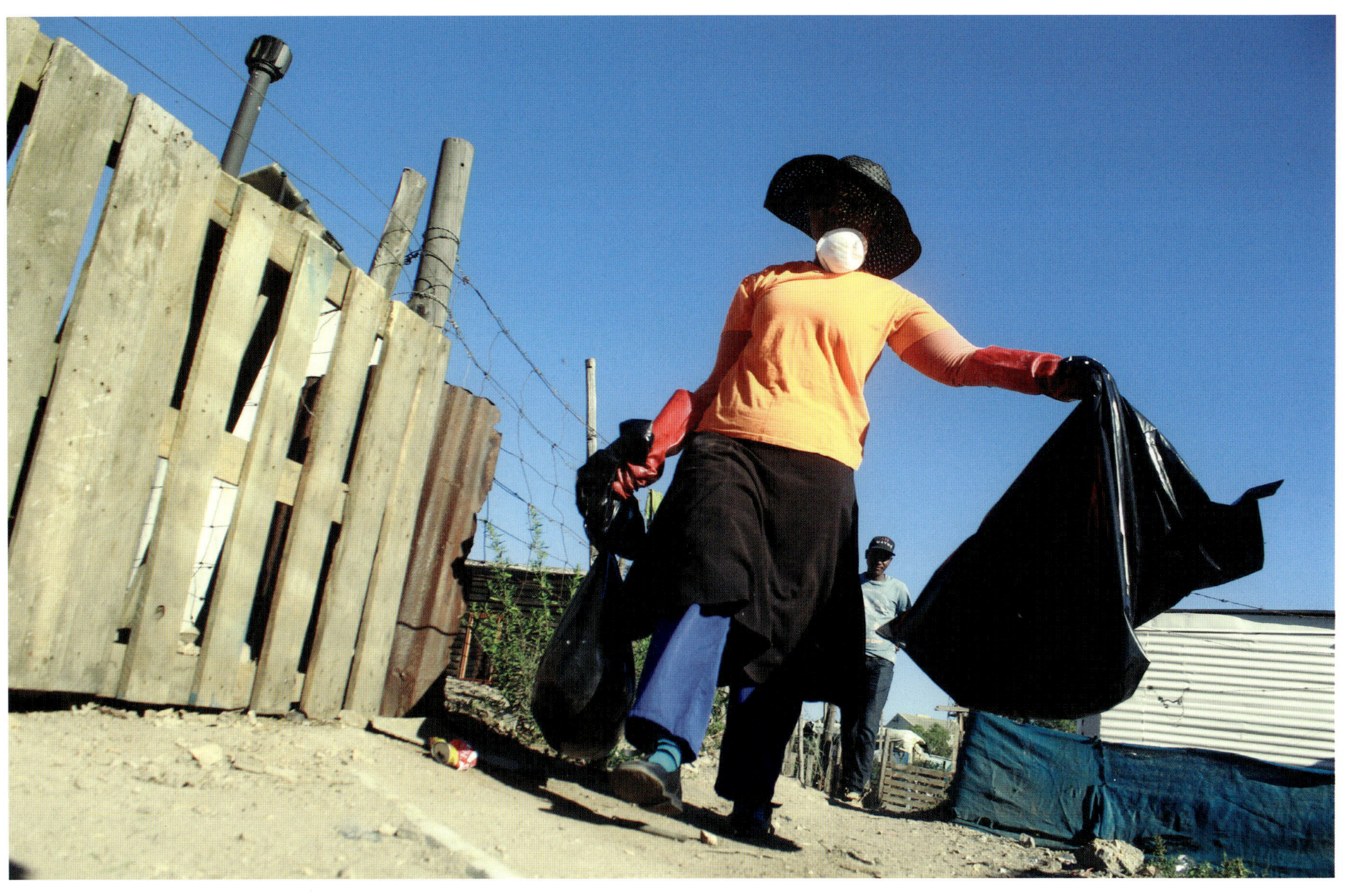

A worker taking black bags containing faeces to a designated area from where they are then collected after a couple of hours; they lie in the open where children are exposed to the flies, germs and smell.

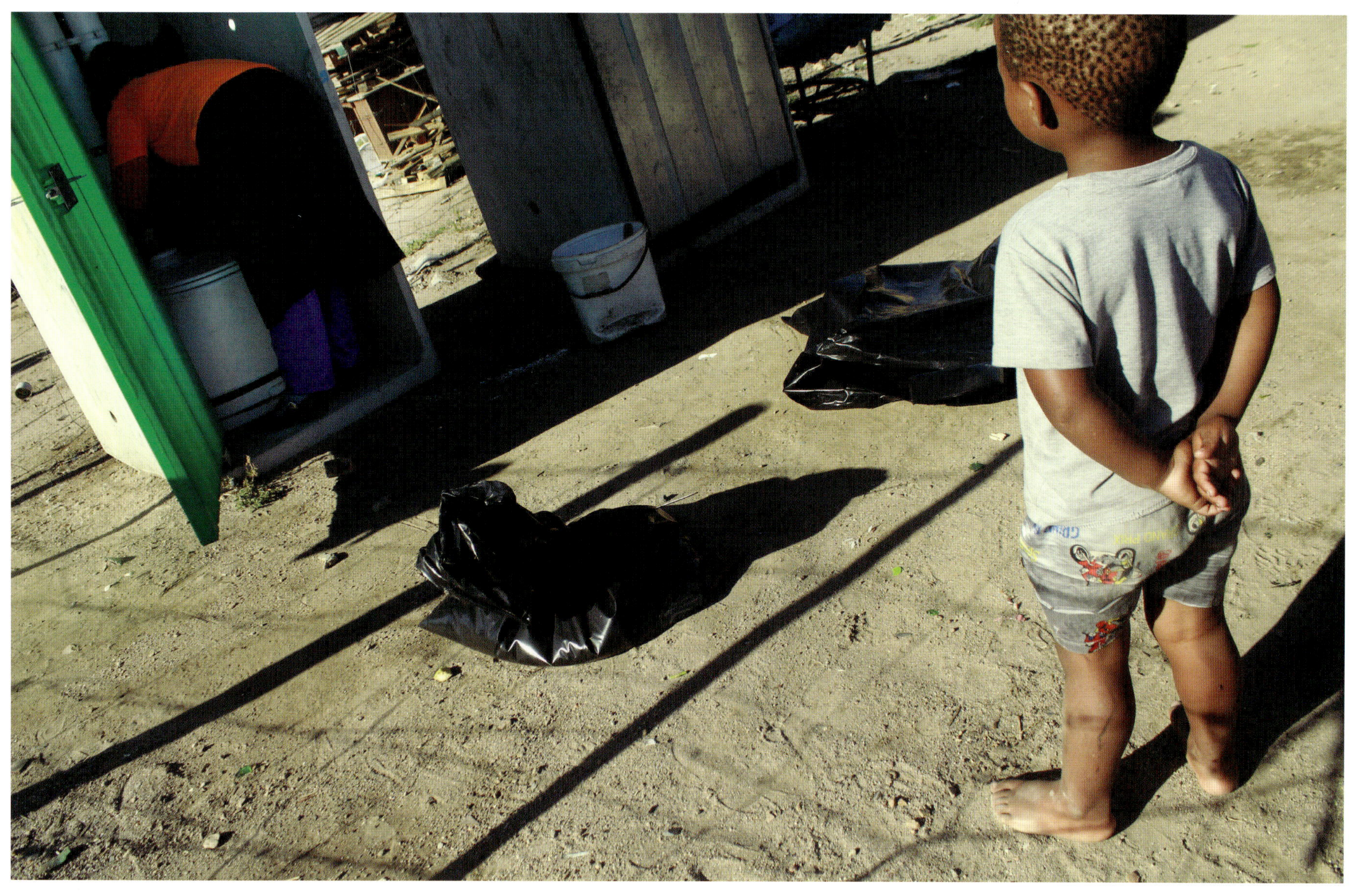

A child watches on as a contract worker collects faeces from communal toilets.

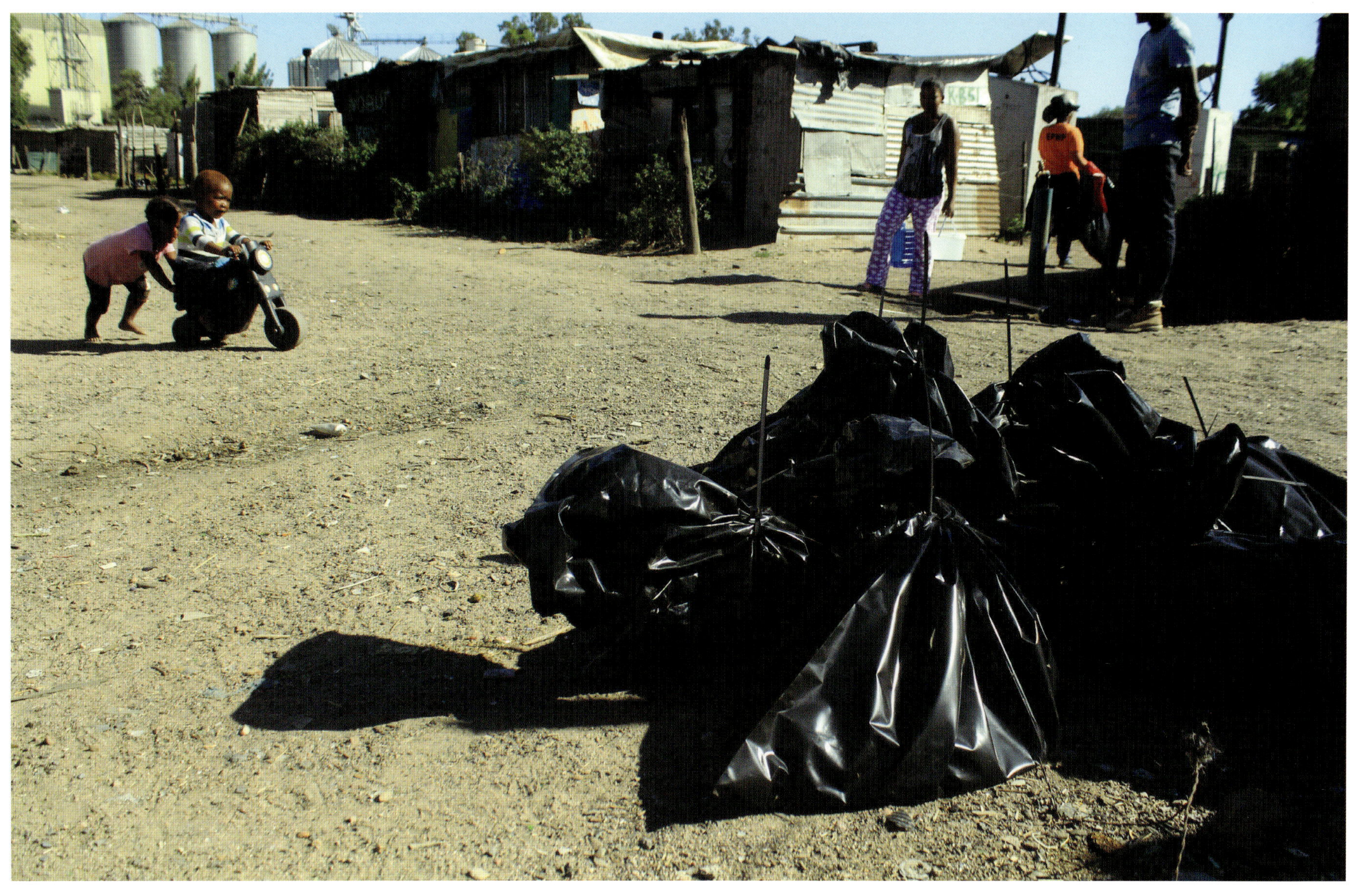

The community, including children, are exposed to faeces collected in black bags.

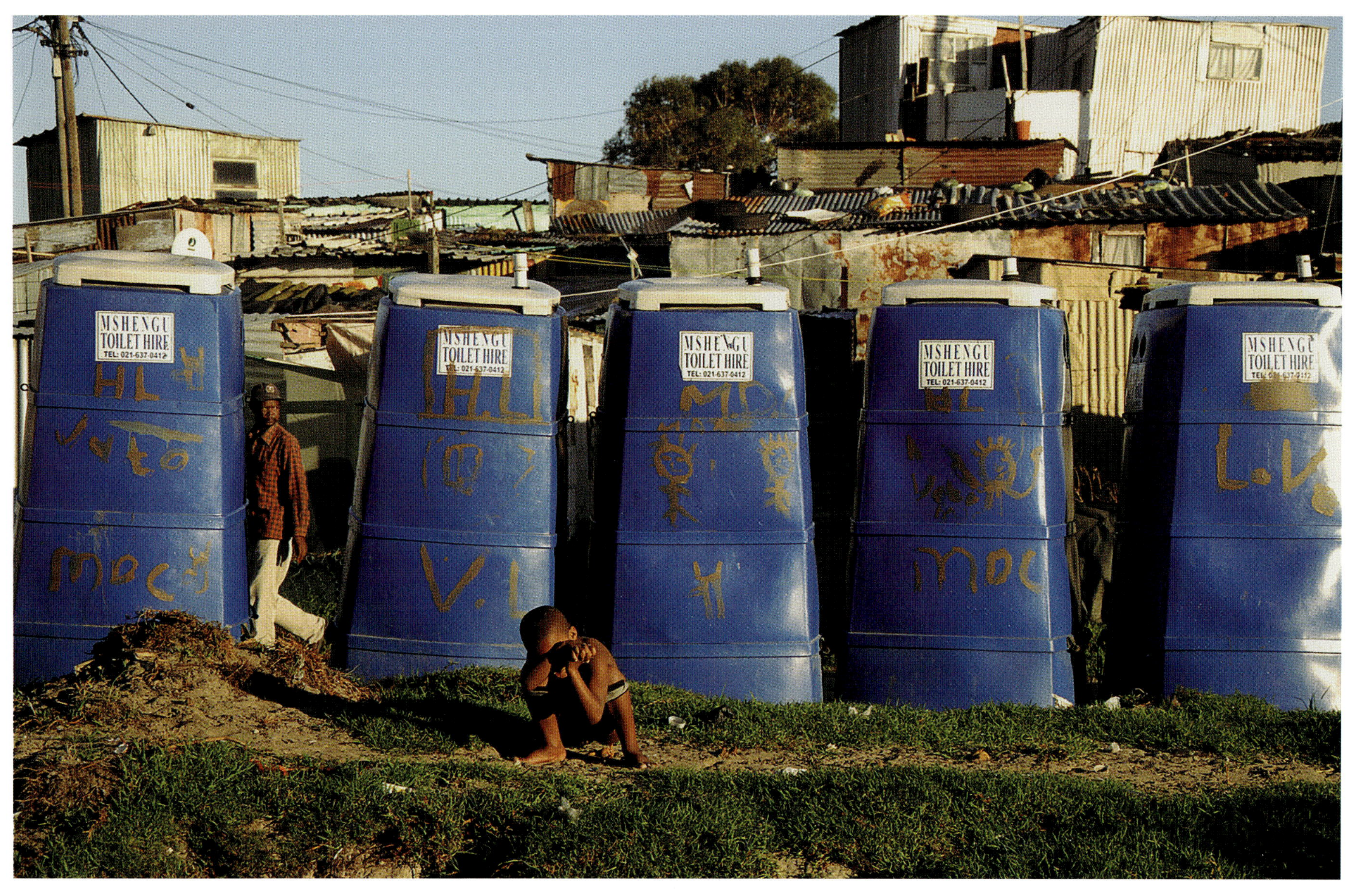

A young boy defecating behind the Mshengu toilets. Many communal
toilets are locked or in a bad state to be used, Site C, Khayelitsha.

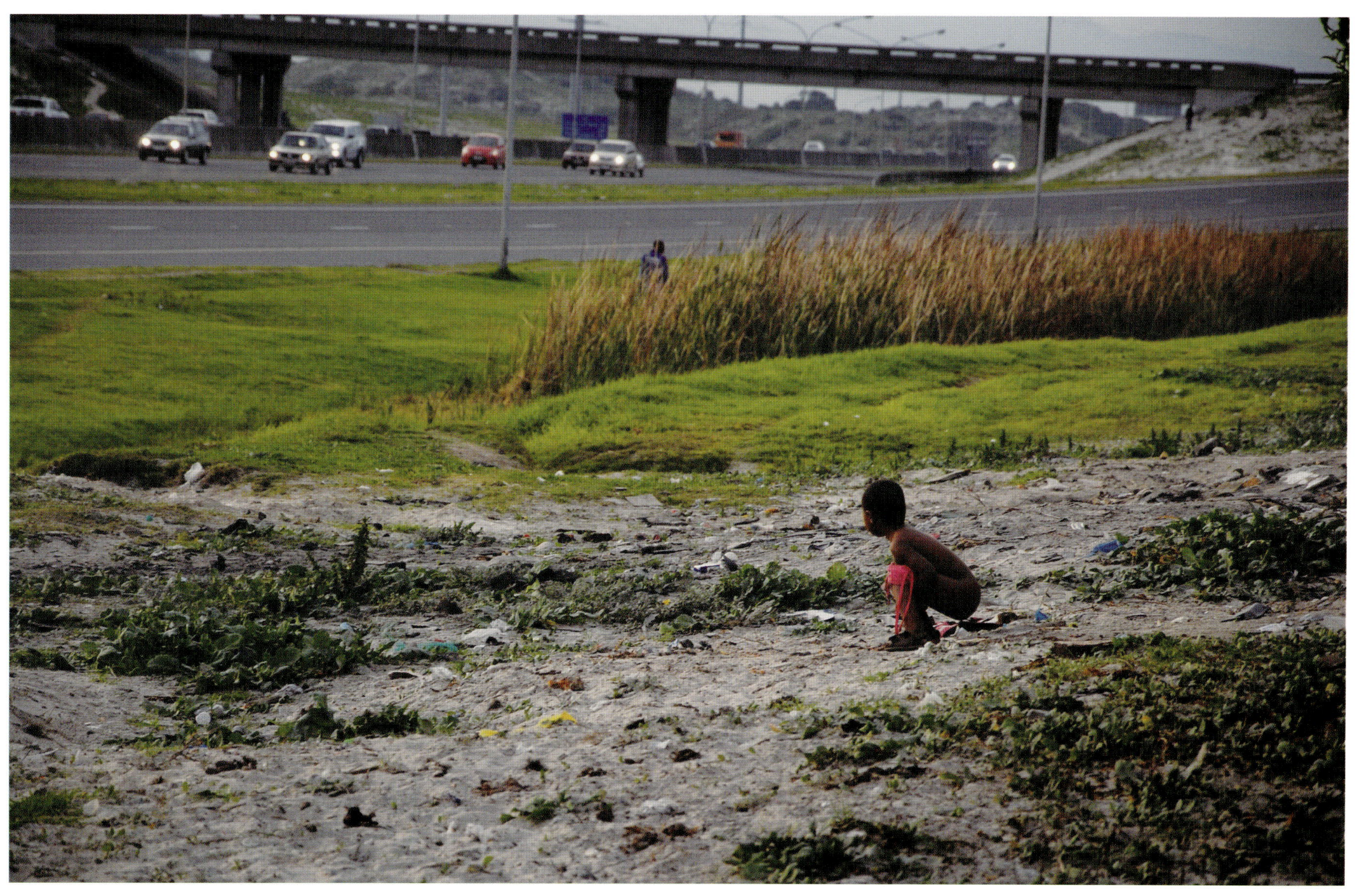

A young girl defecating along the N2 highway, Khayelitsha.

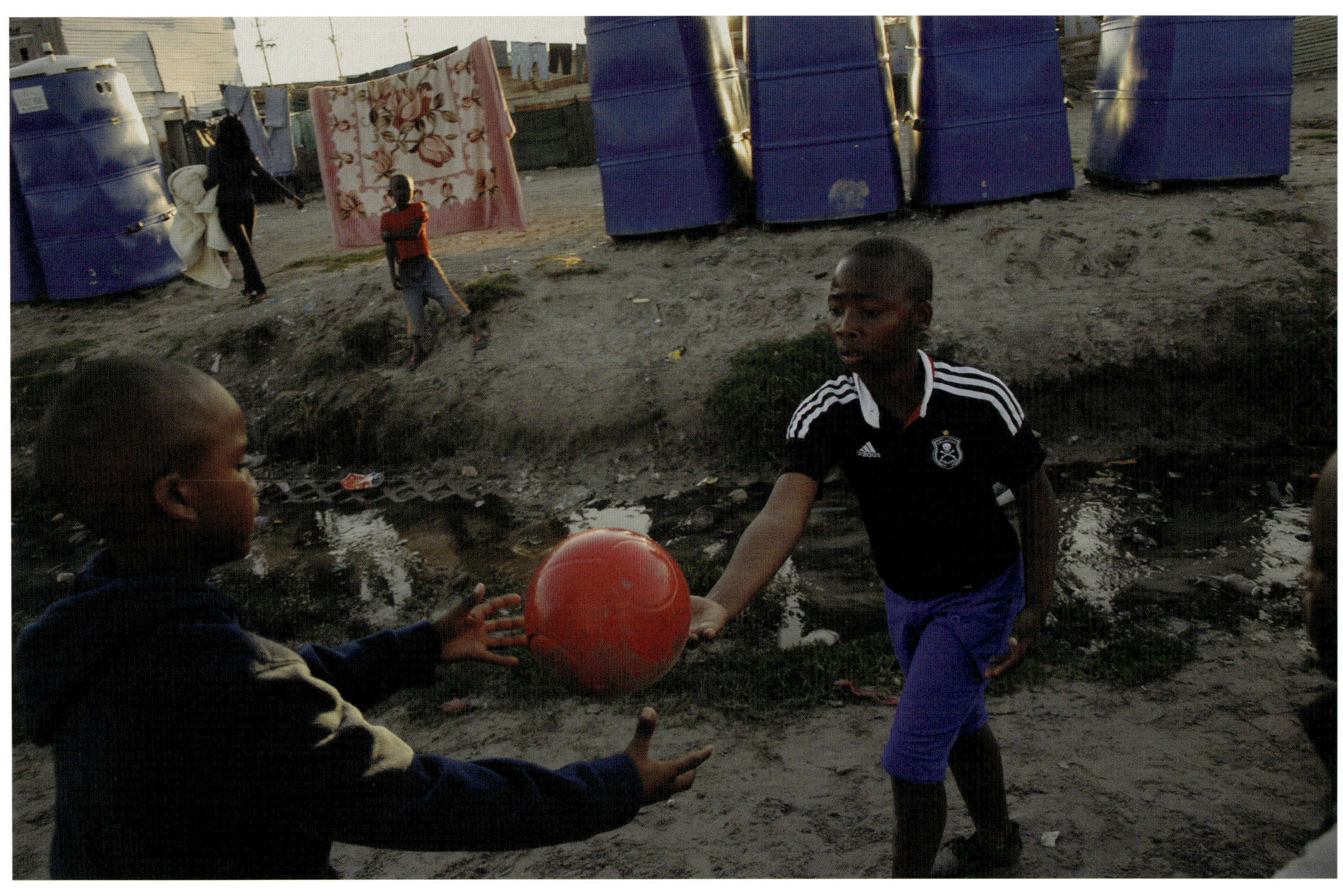

Boys playing; behind them is stagnant water from the public
communal toilet, Site C, Khayelitsha.

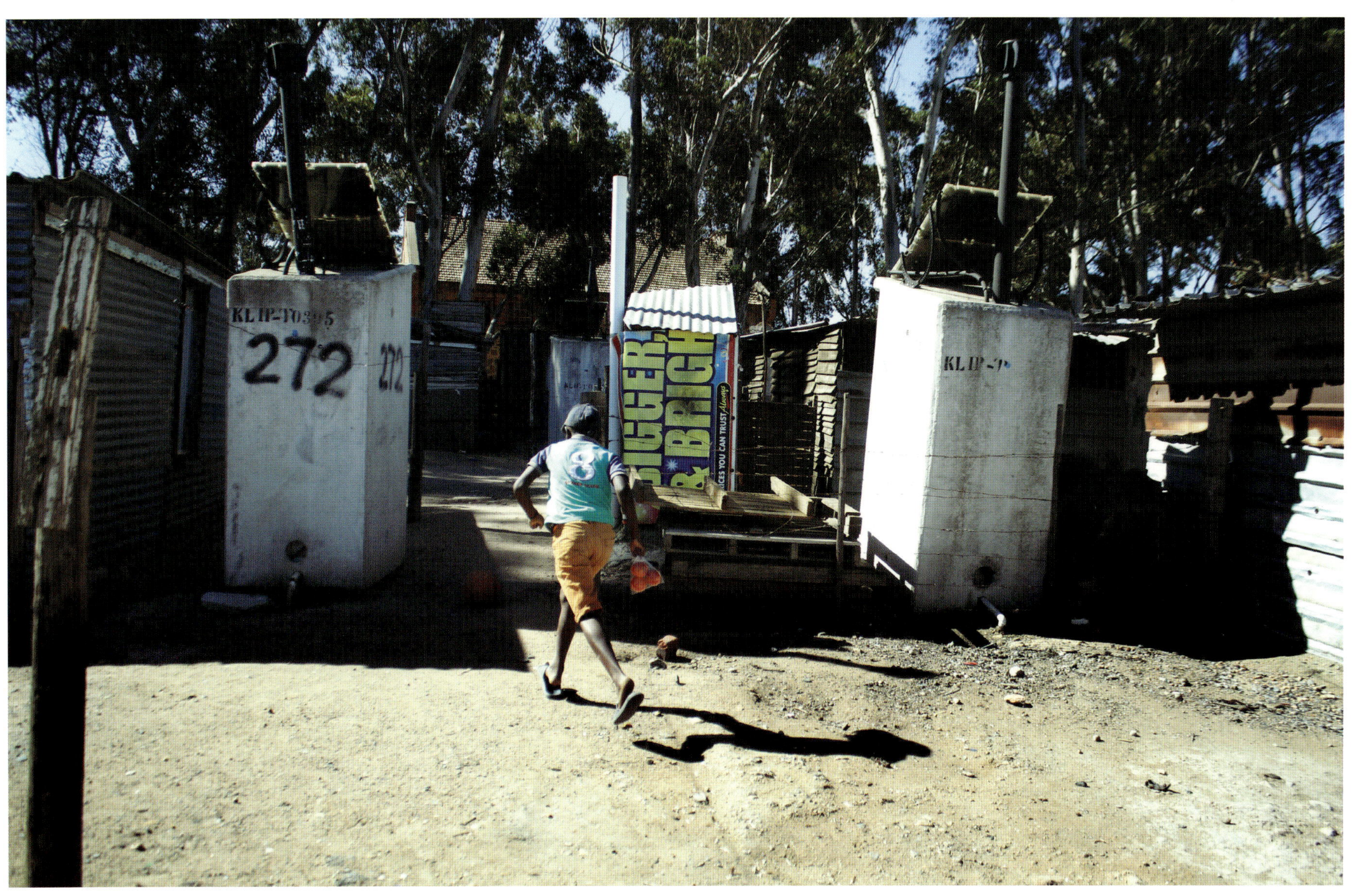

Communal toilets used as soccer poles, Klipheuwel.

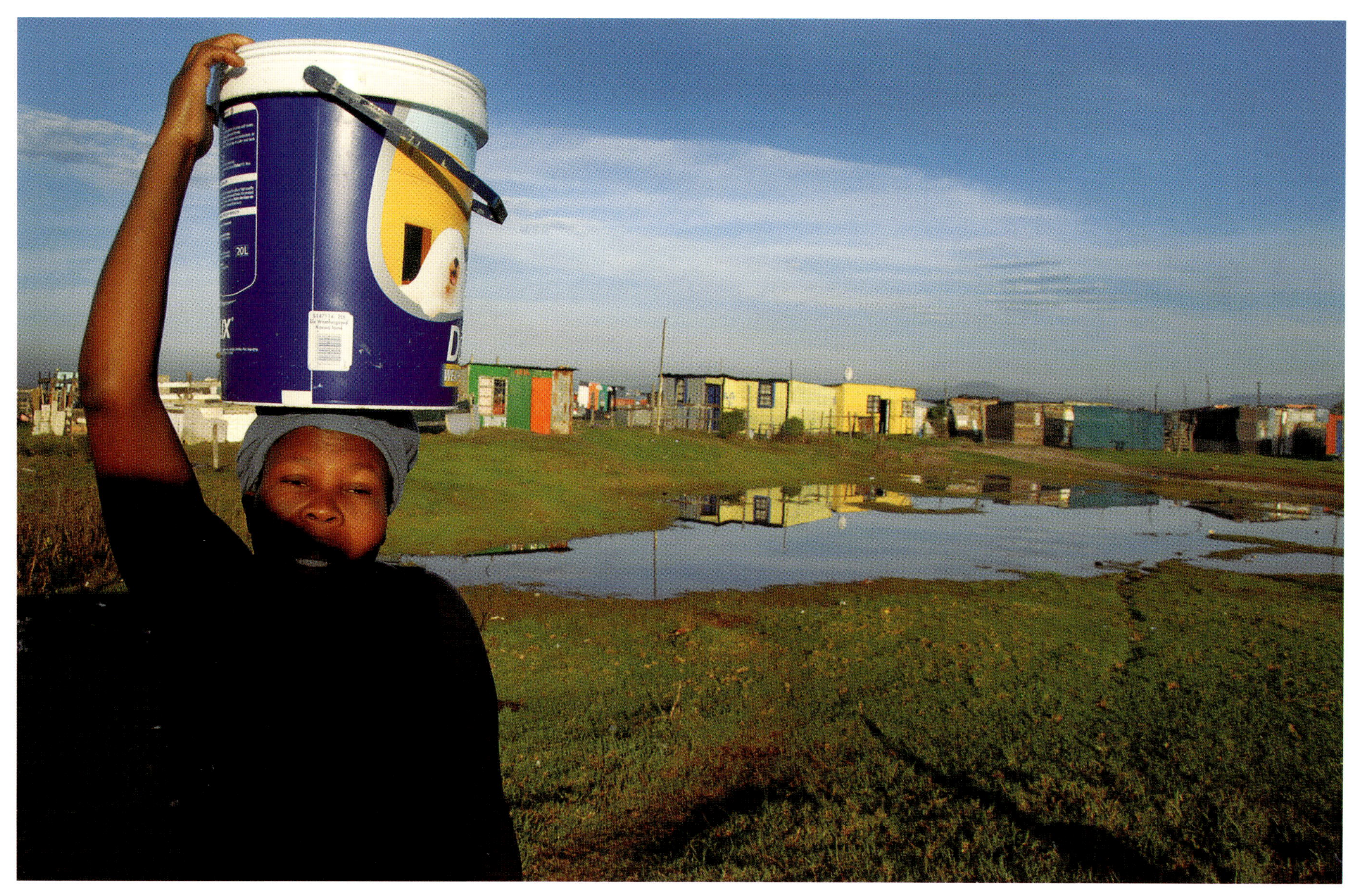

A woman collecting water from a communal tap, Mfuleni.

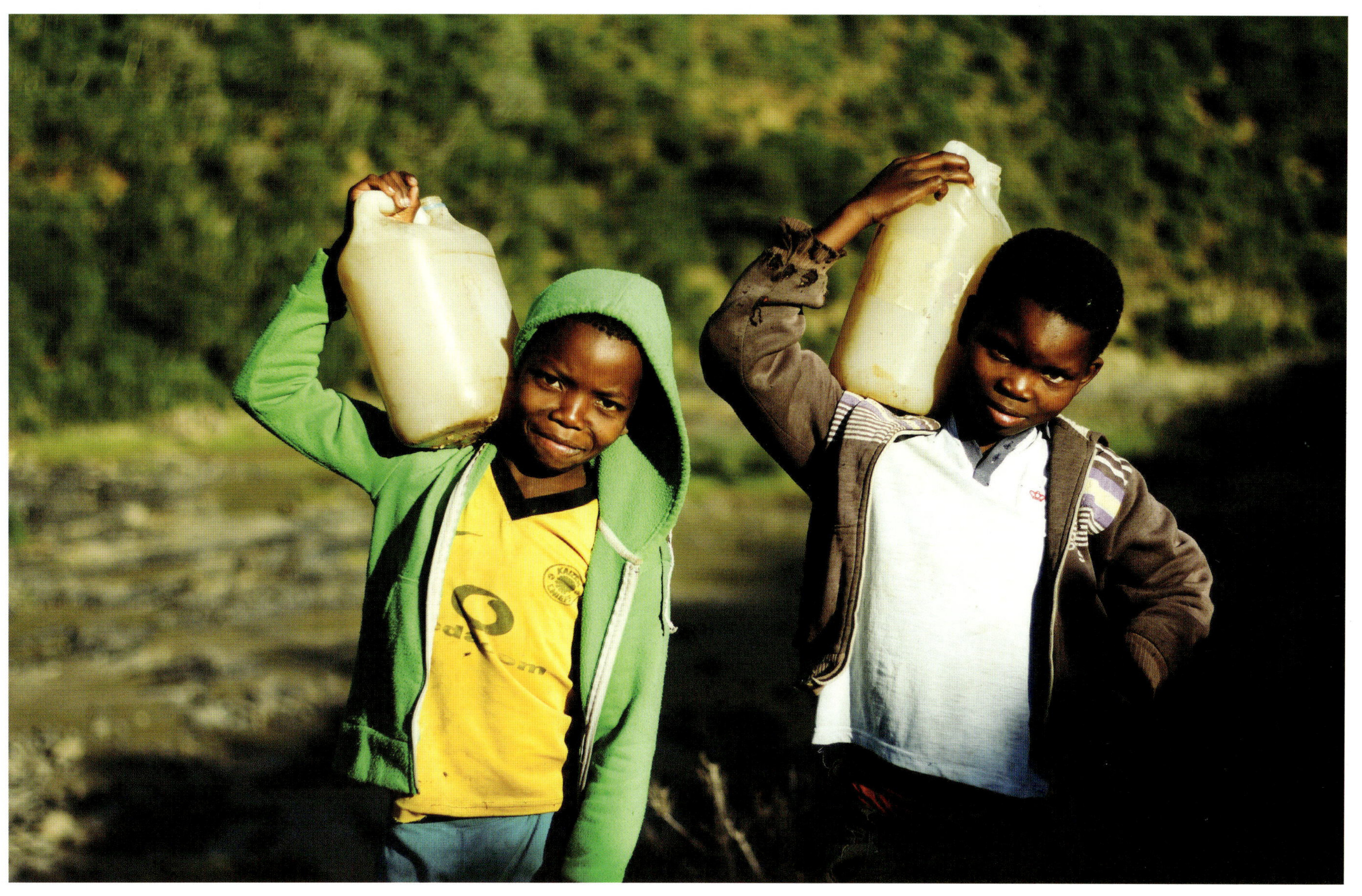

Ongezile Mkwehla and Siya Wandisa pose for a photo after collecting
fresh water from the Imzimvubu River, Eastern Cape.

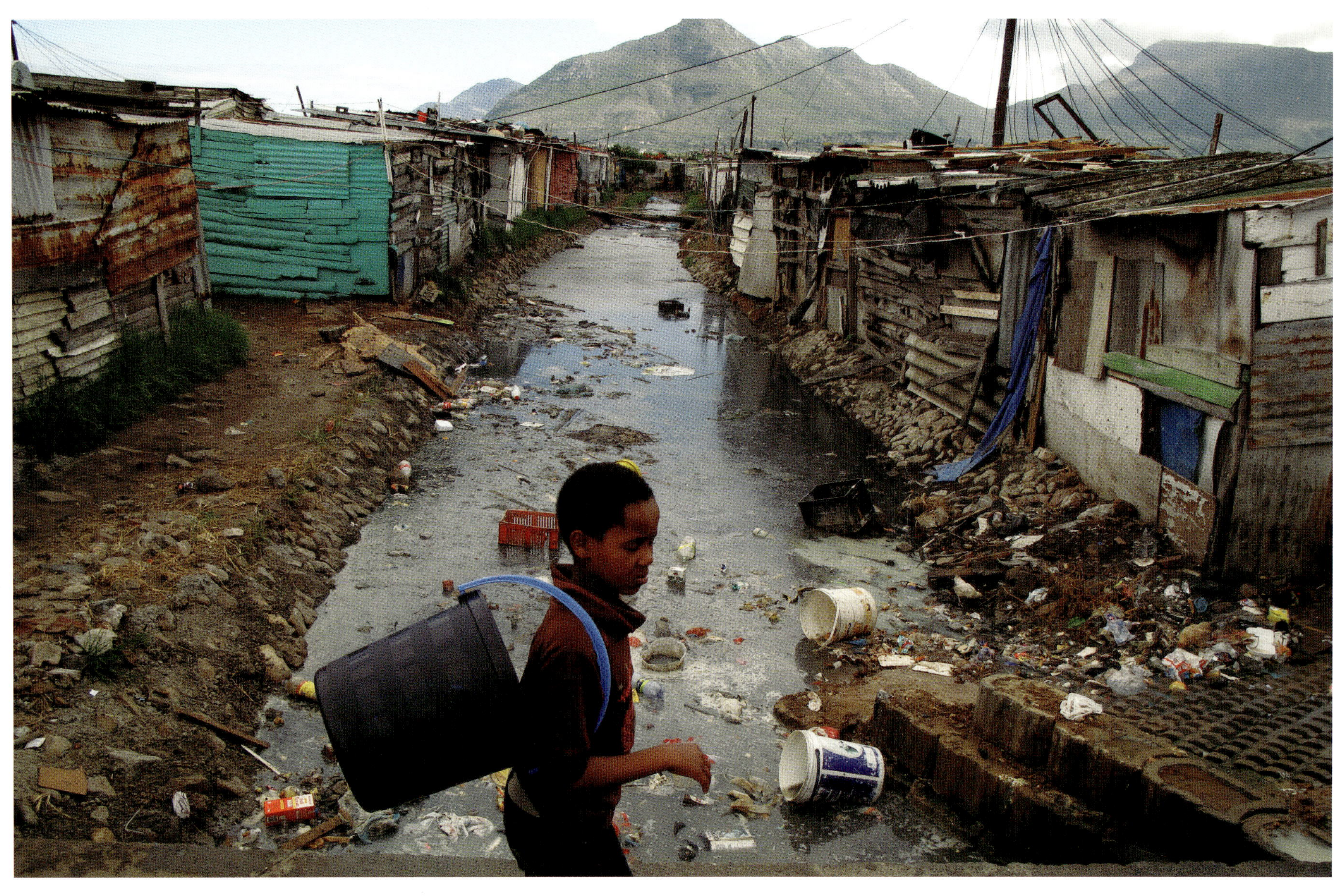

A woman walking past an unbearably dirty canal on her way to collect fresh water in Hout Bay, Masiphumelele.

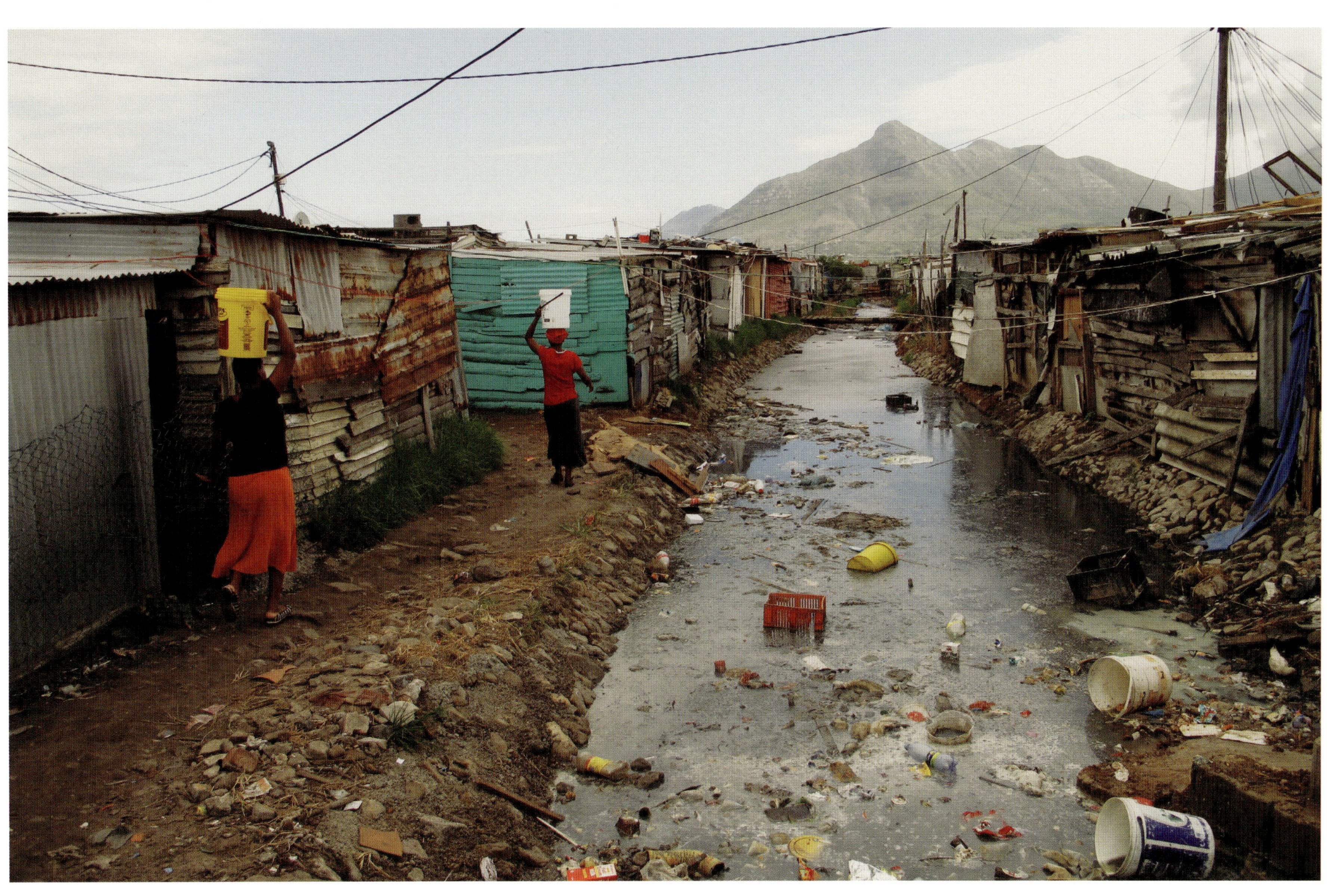

Two ladies on their way back from getting fresh water from a communal tap in Hout Bay, Masiphumelele.

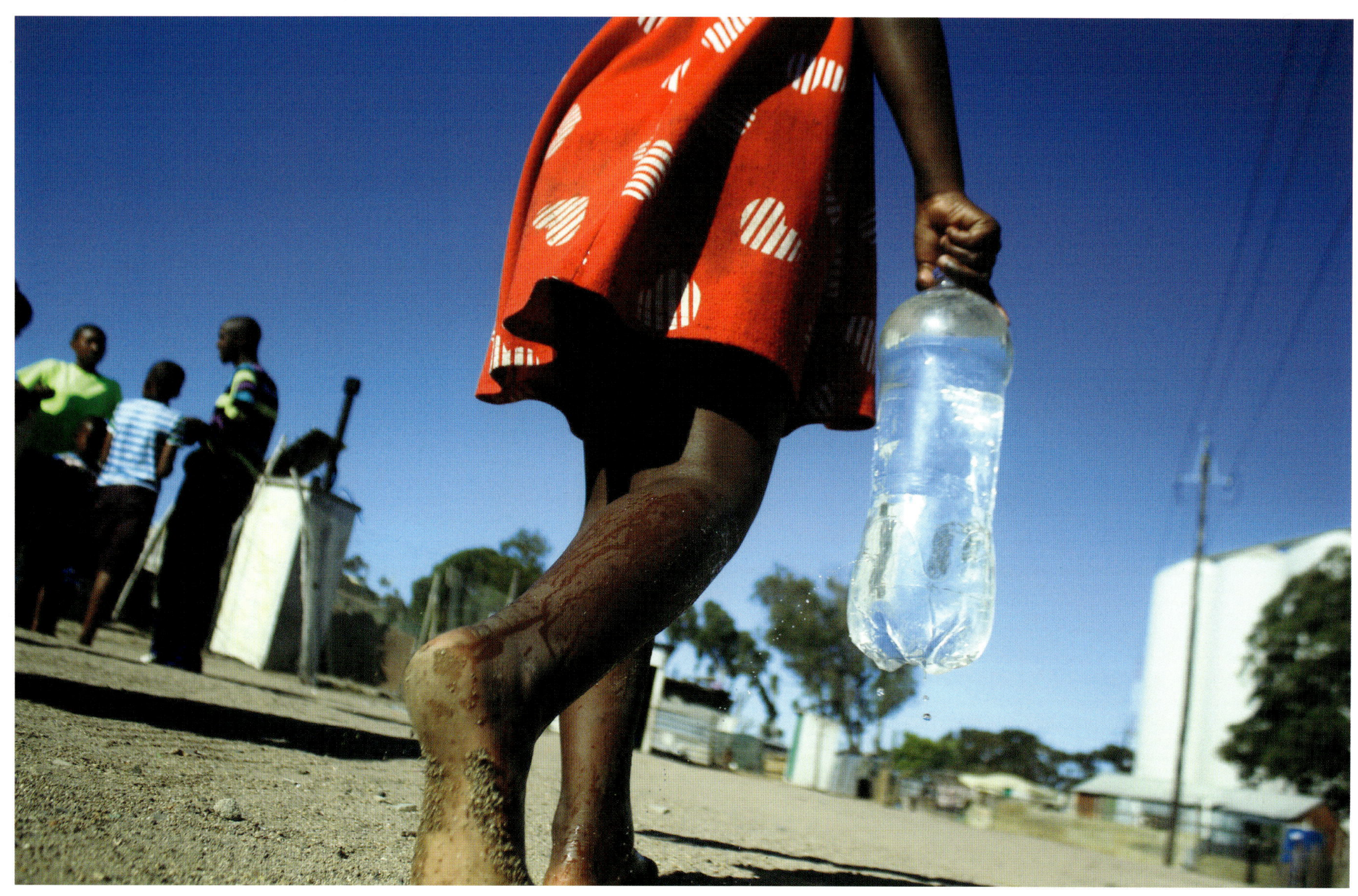

A hot summer's day in Klipheuwel.

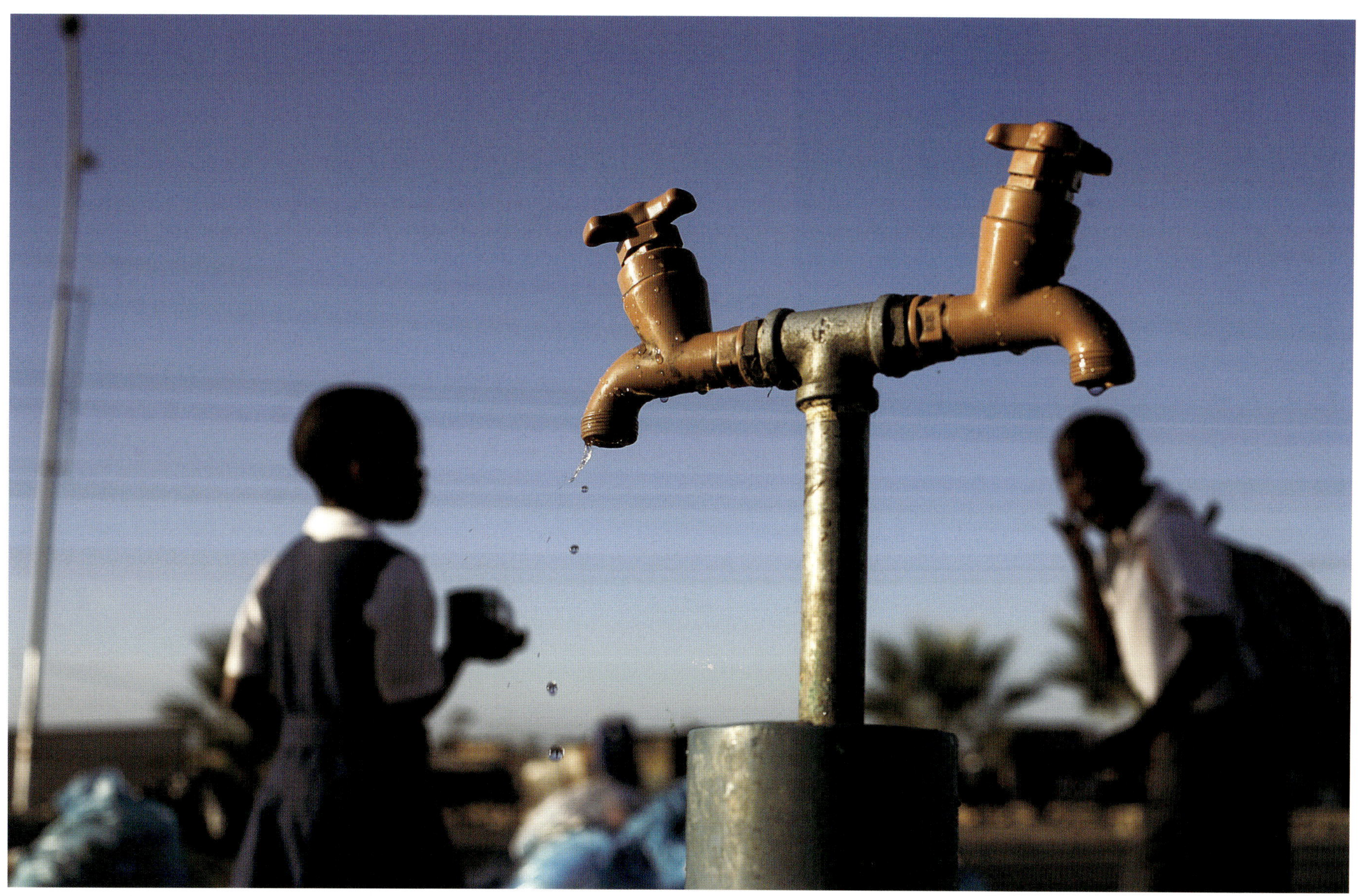

Two kids next to a communal tap in Site C, Khayelitsha.

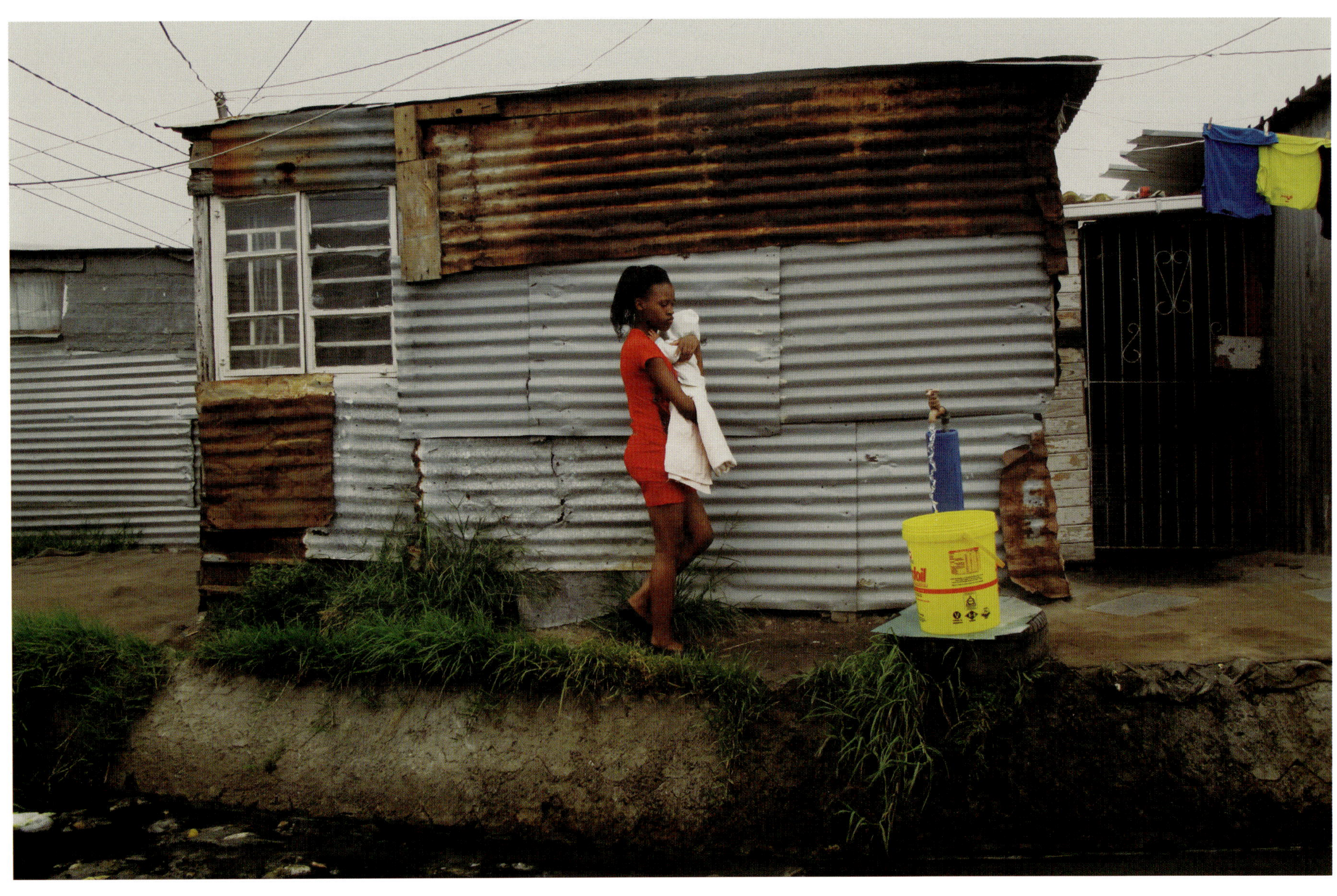

A young girl with a newborn passing a communal tap in Hout
Bay, Masiphumelele.

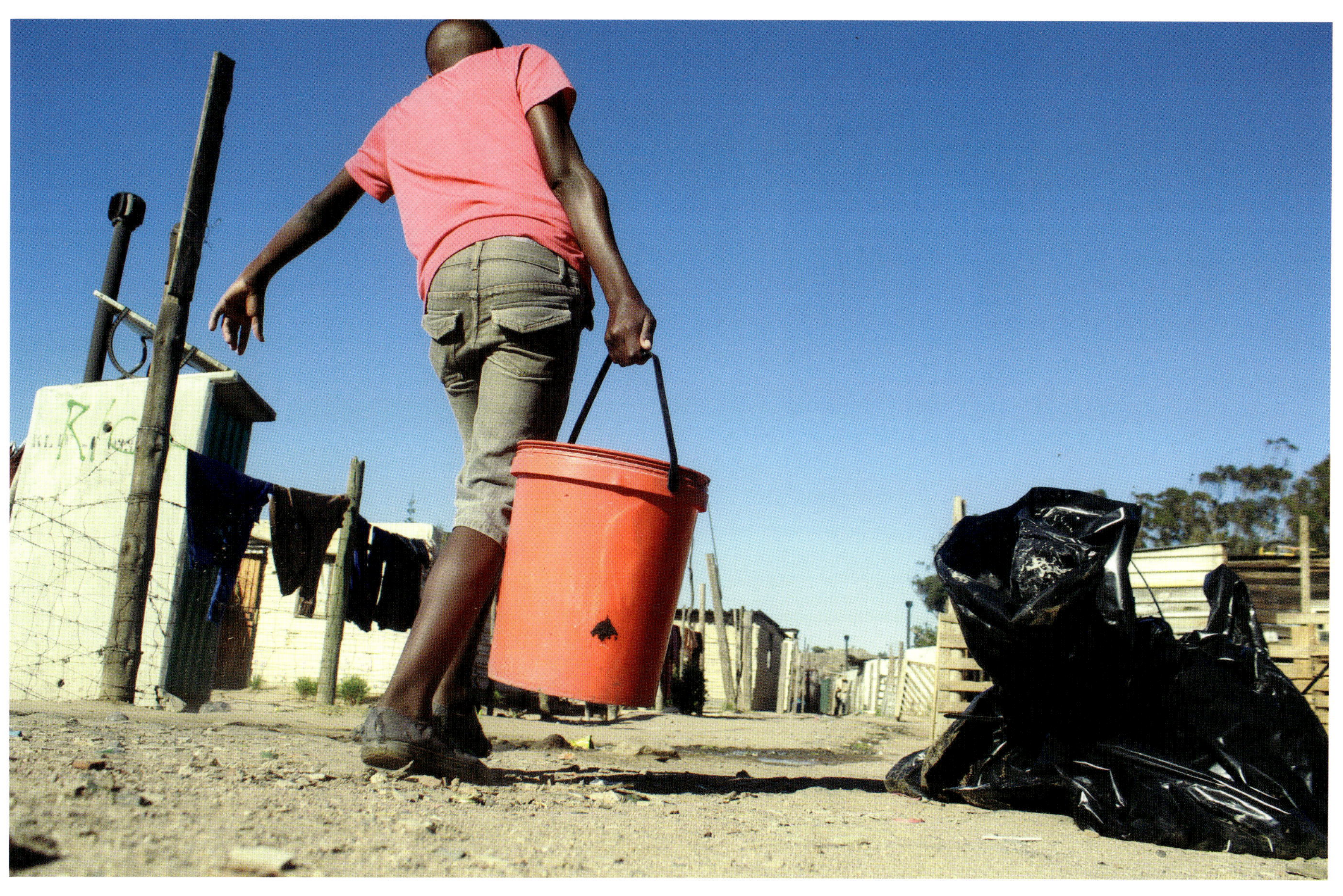

A young man walking past a bag of faeces on his way back from collecting water from a communal tap in Klipheuwel.

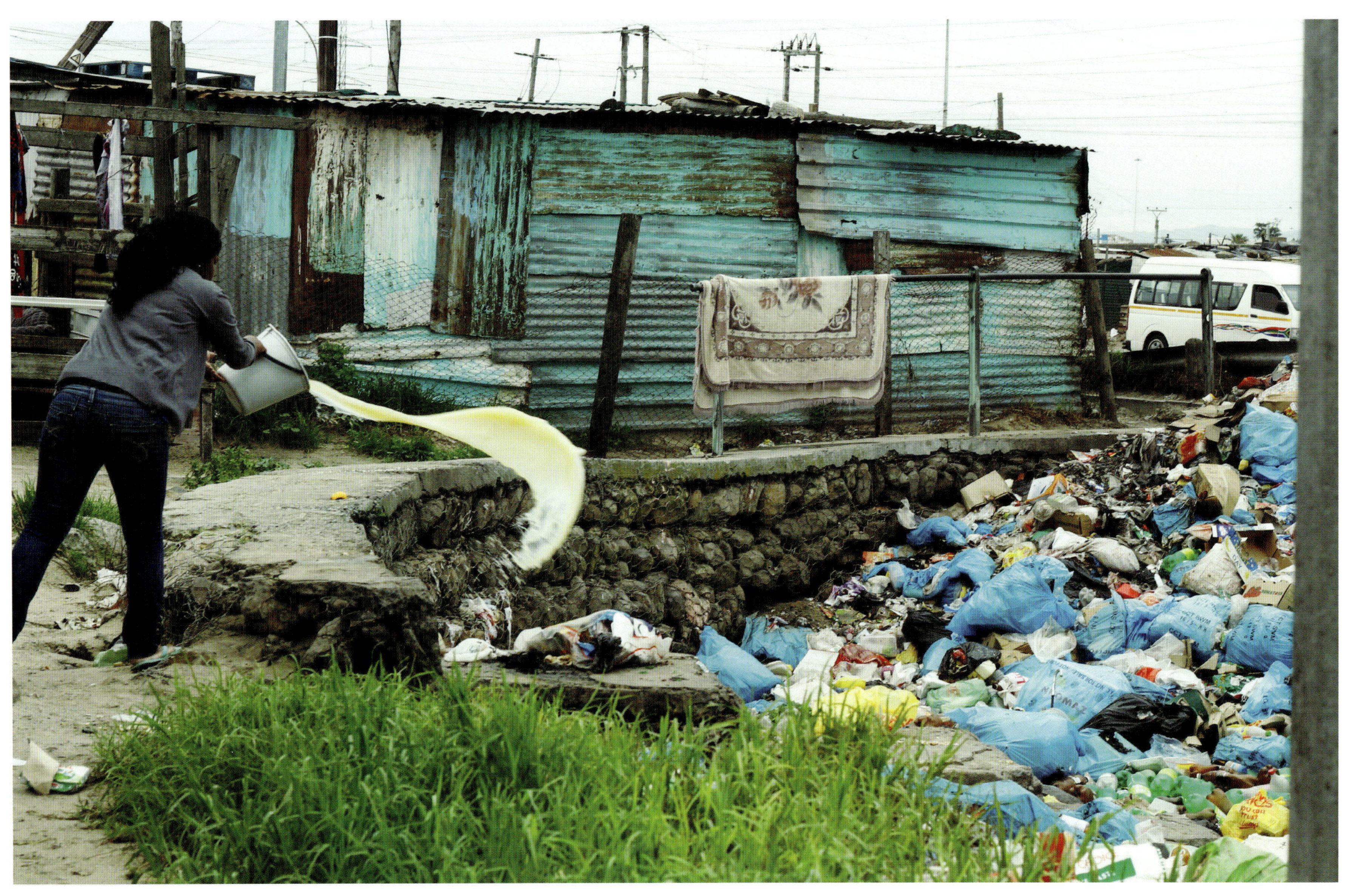

A women throws faeces from a bucket into a garbage dump, Site C, Khayelitsha.

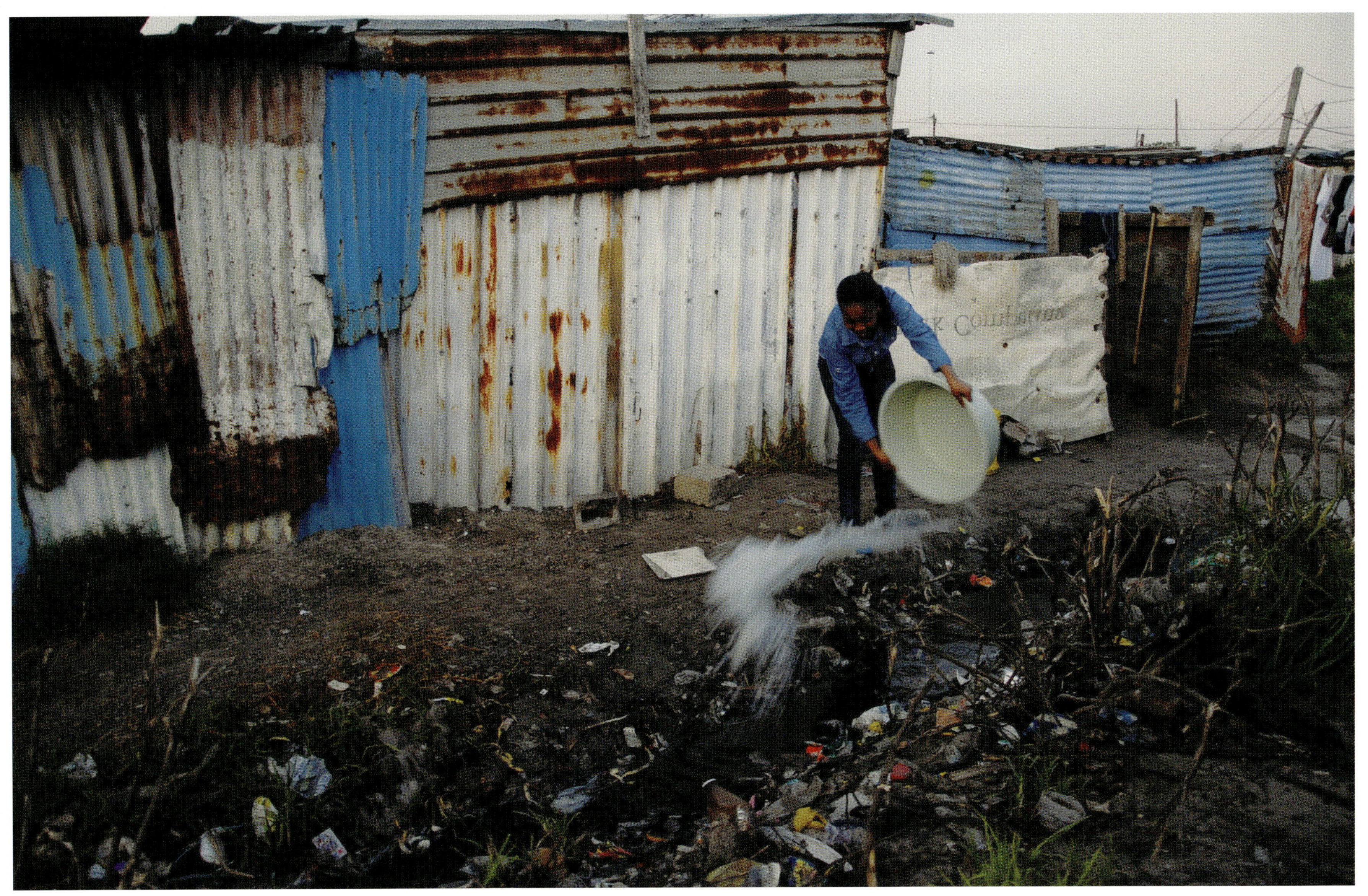

Throwing out bath water, Site C, Khayelitsha.

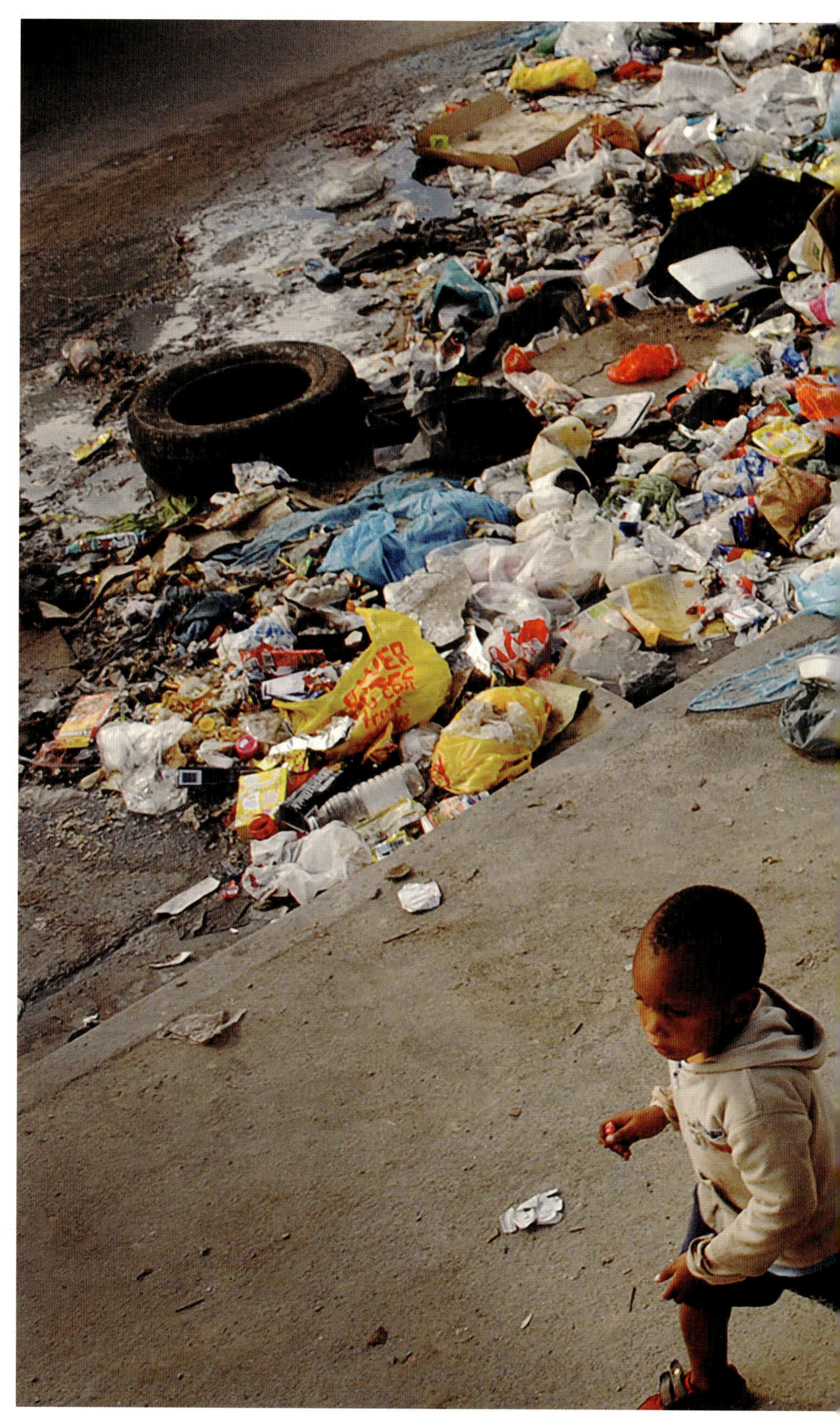

A child running past a dumping site in Philippi.

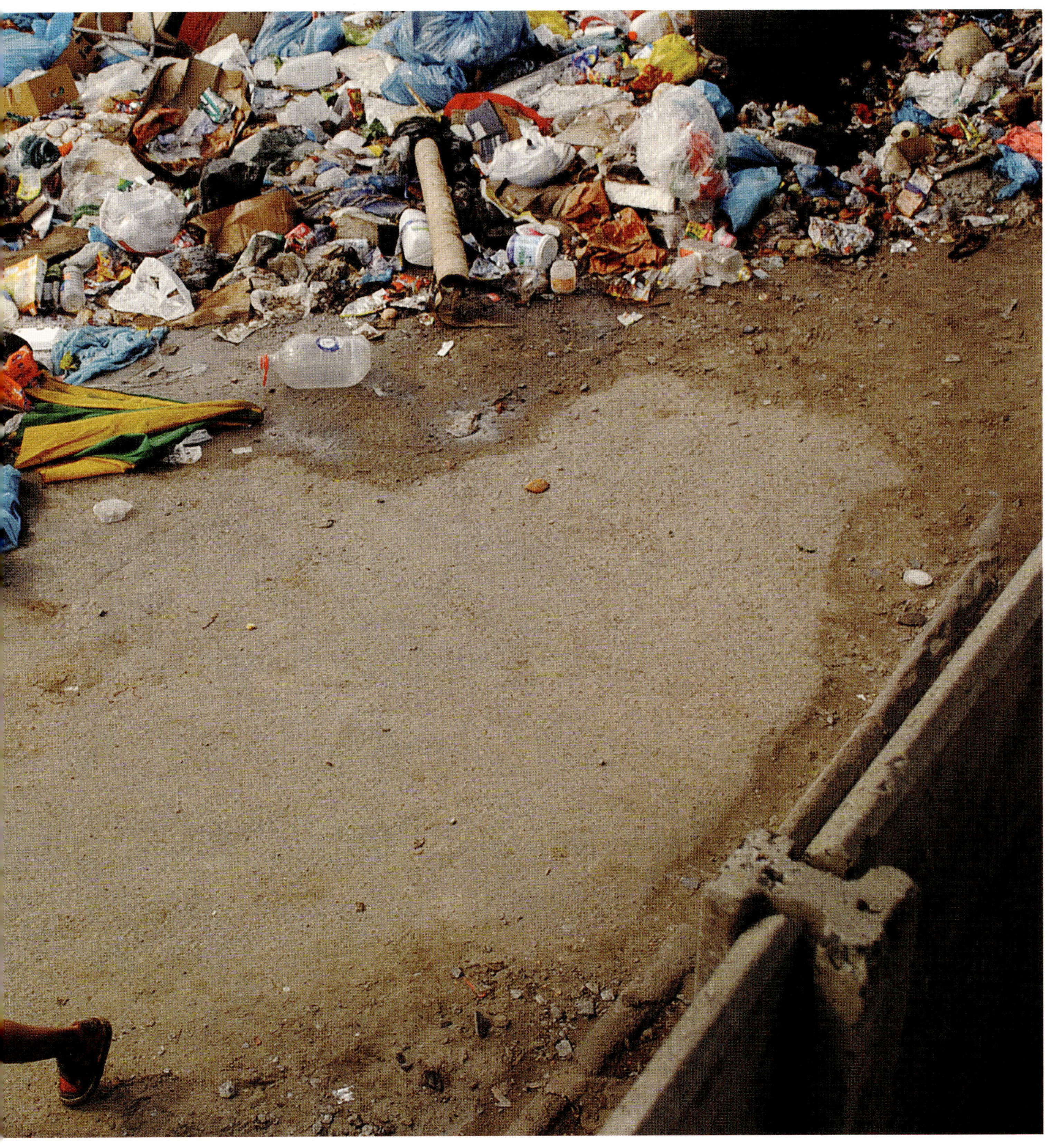

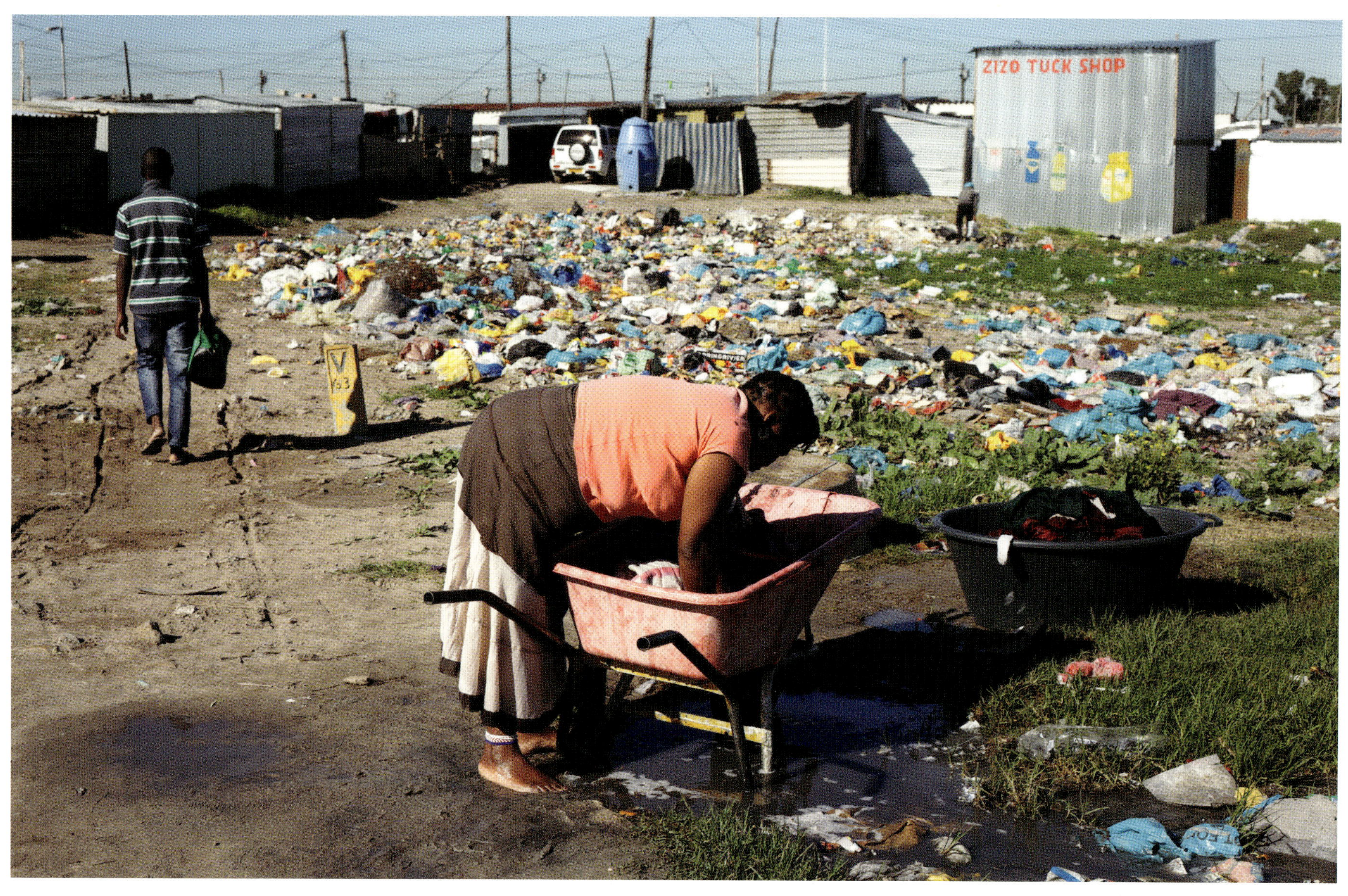

Nomvisiswano Lutwetsha washing clothes in the open, Marikana.

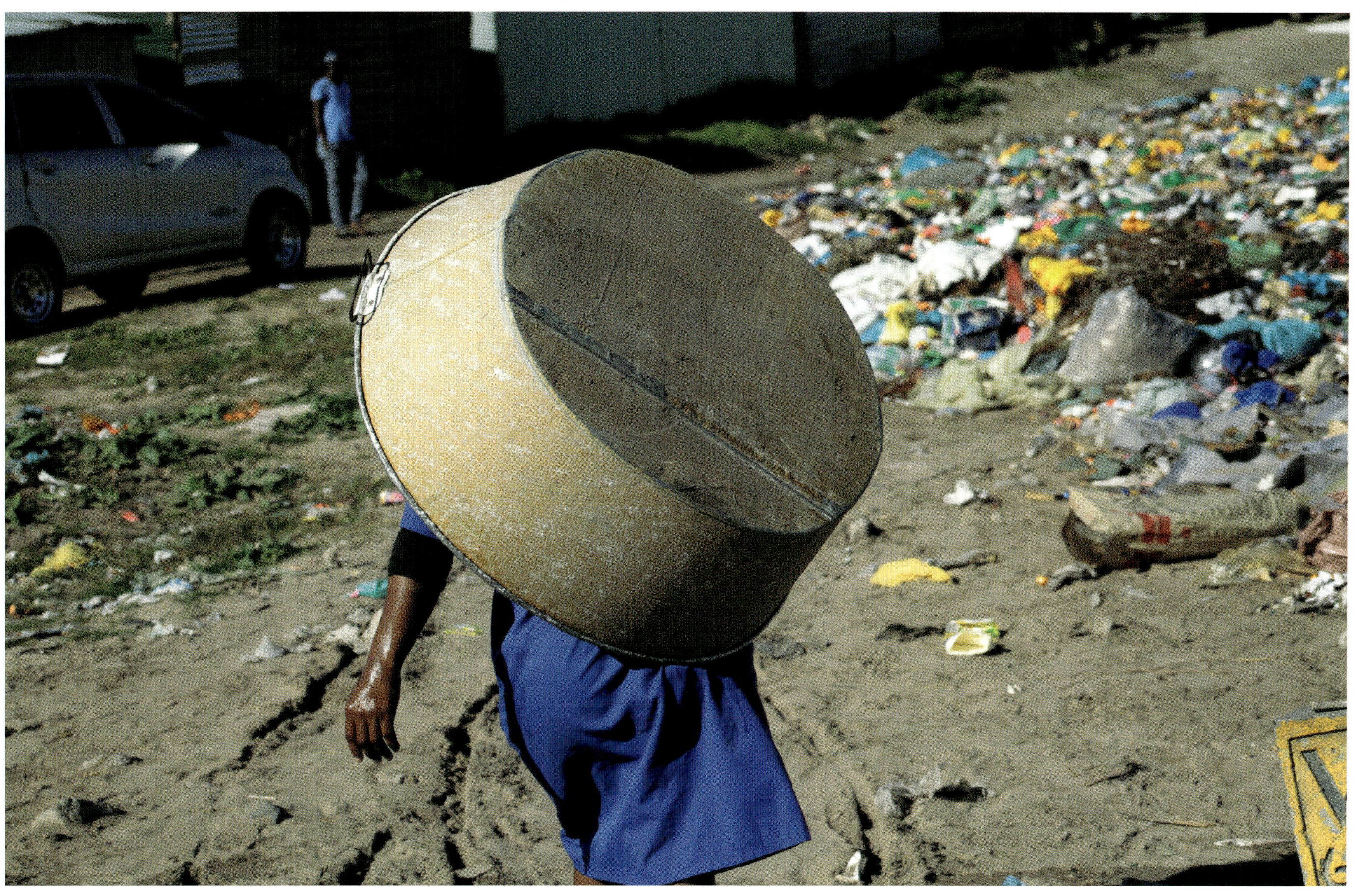

Walking home after doing laundry in Marikana.

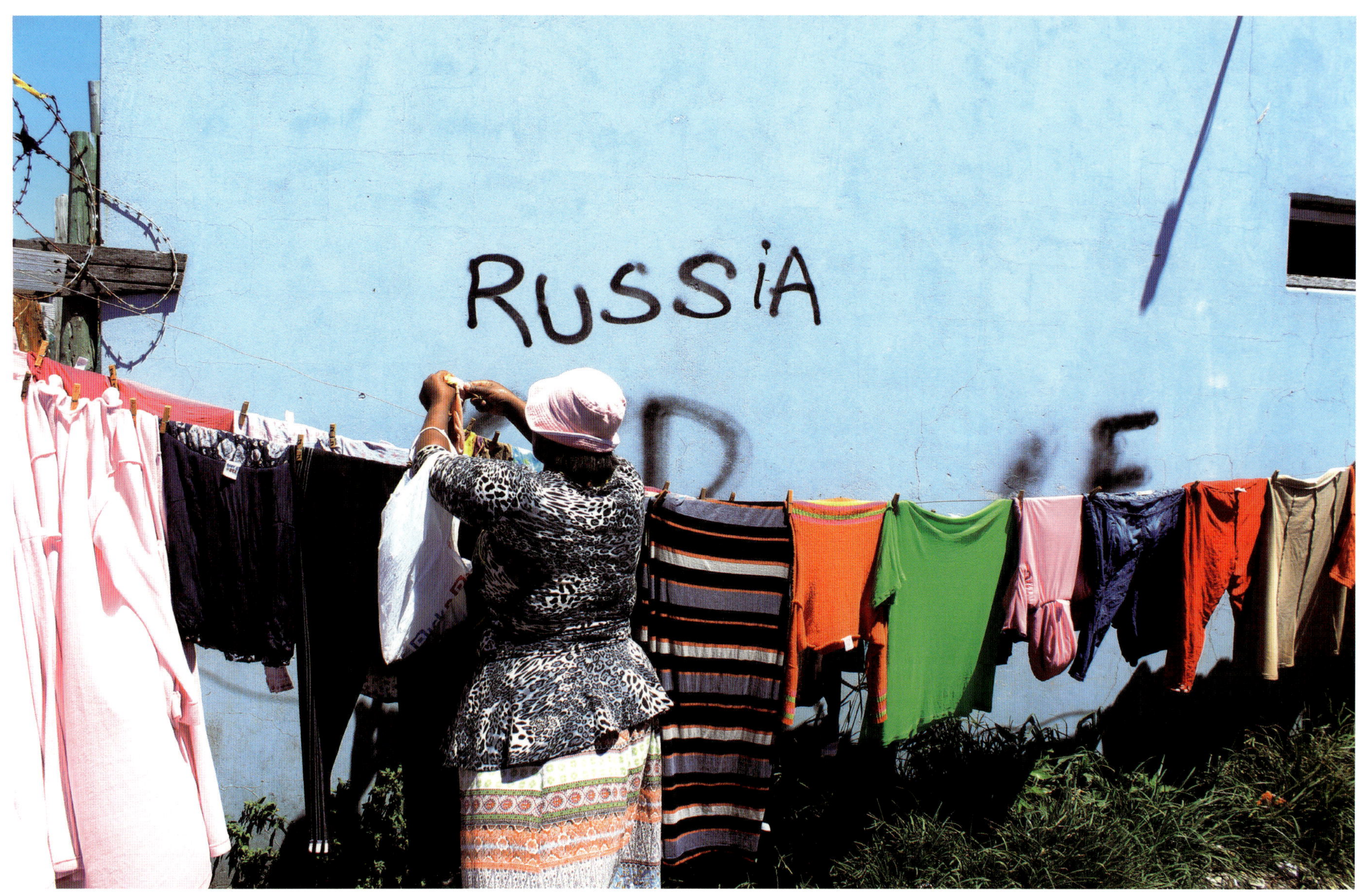

Hanging up washing, Hout Bay, Masiphumelele.

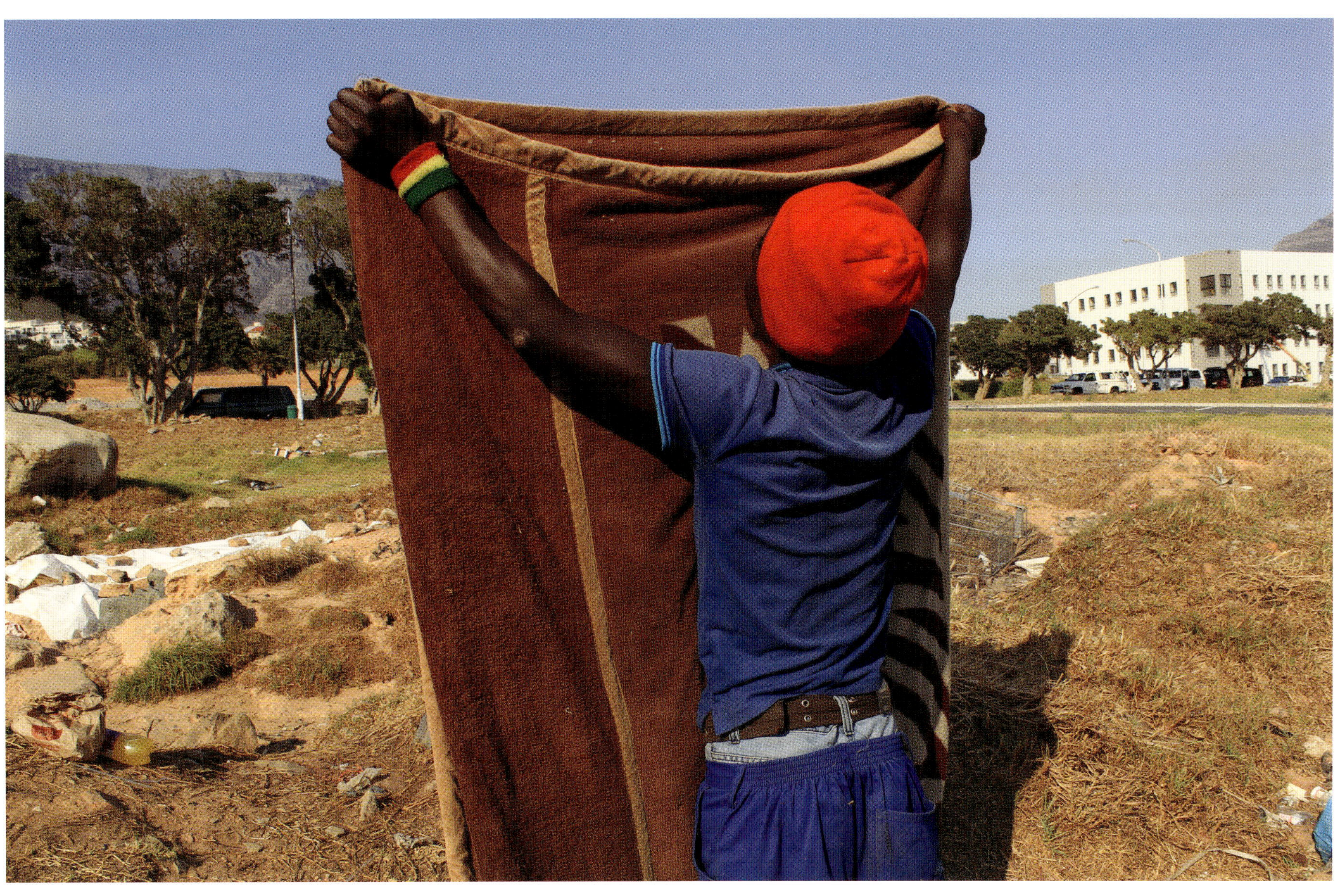

A Rastafarian from Limpopo who came to Cape Town in the hope of getting a job. He lives with other street dwellers on the open fields of District Six, which was once a multi-racial area.

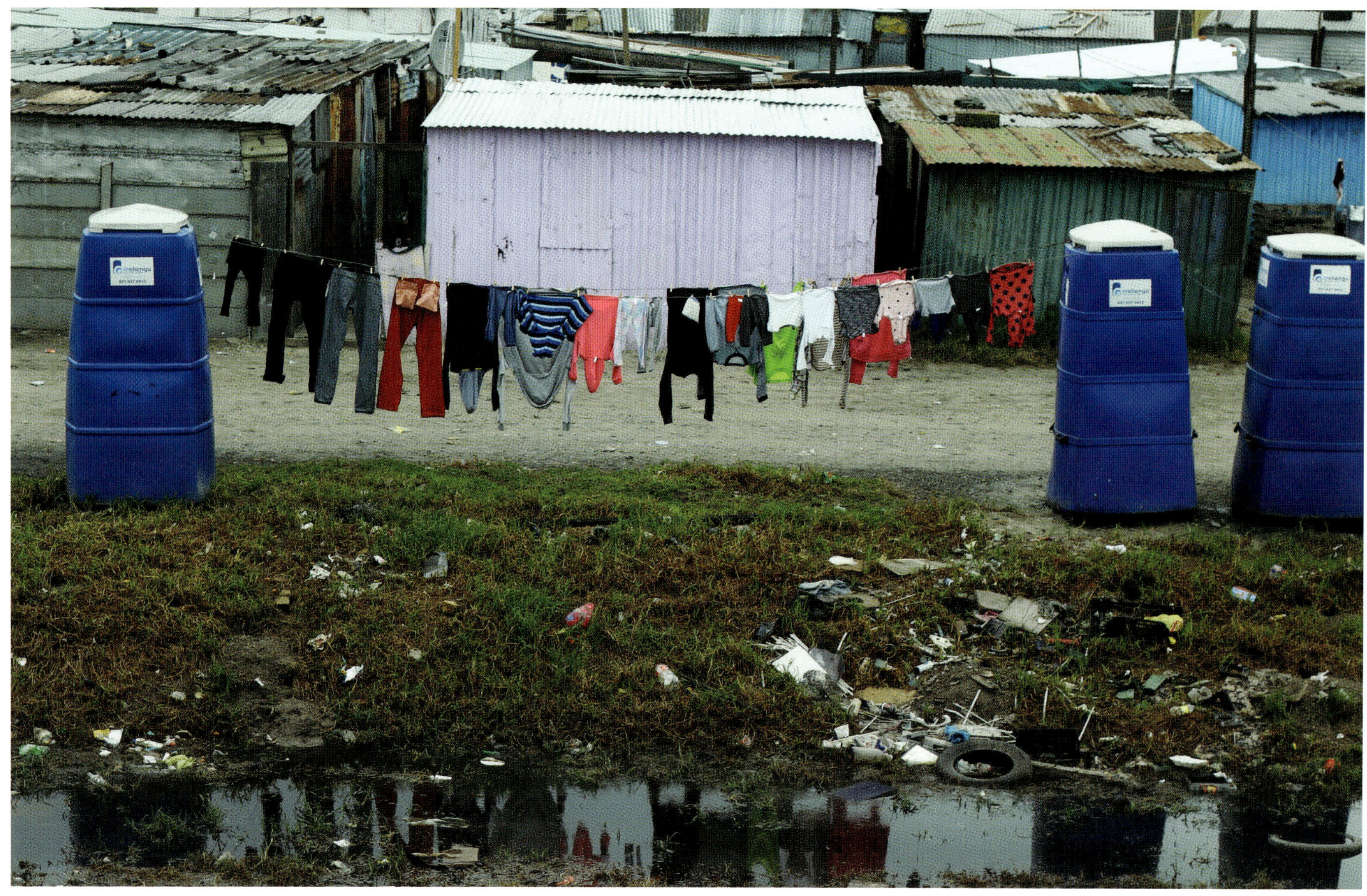

Perfect clothing line.

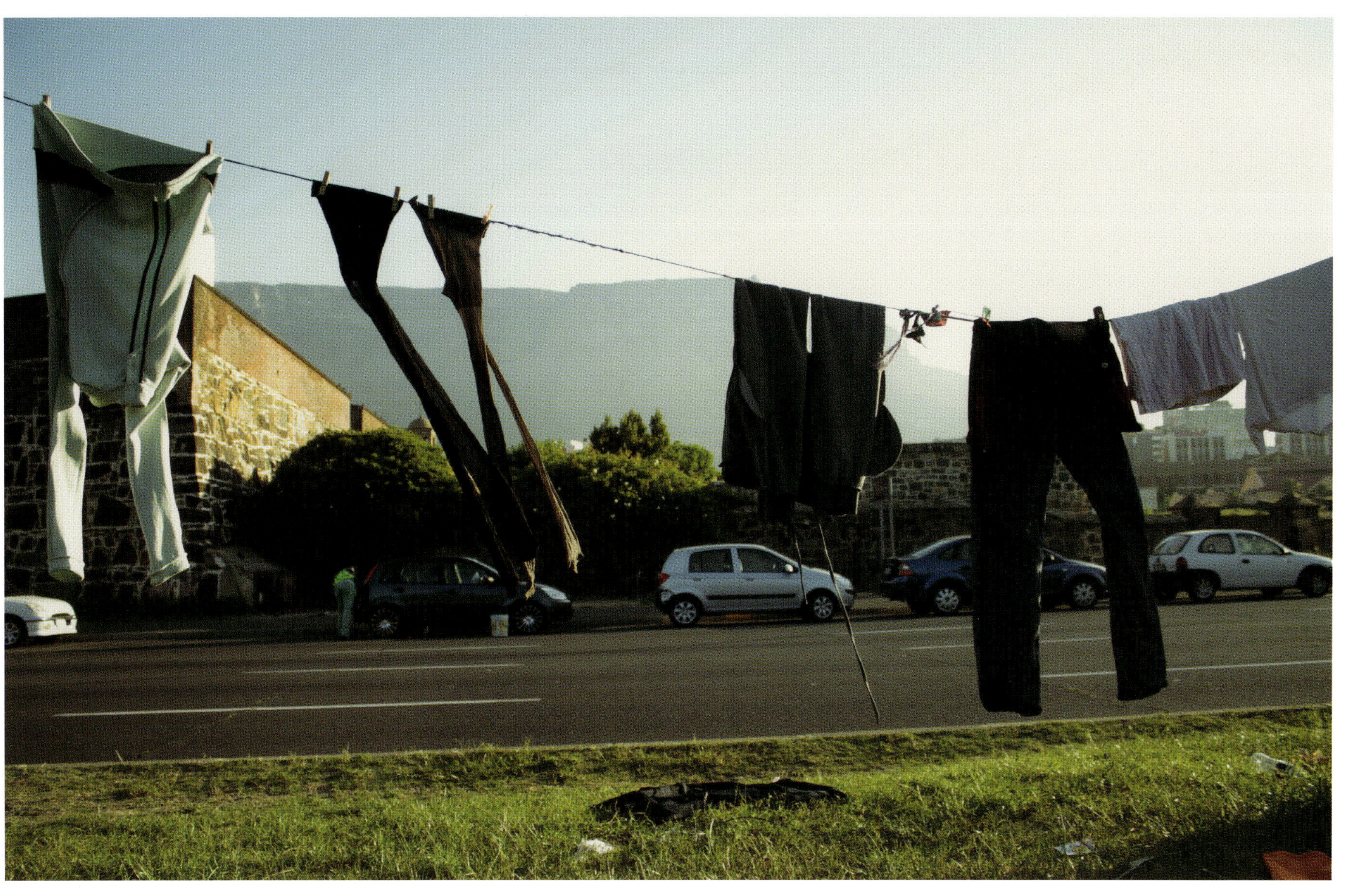

A row of clothing hanging opposite Castle of Good Hope,
which attracts visitors from all over the world.

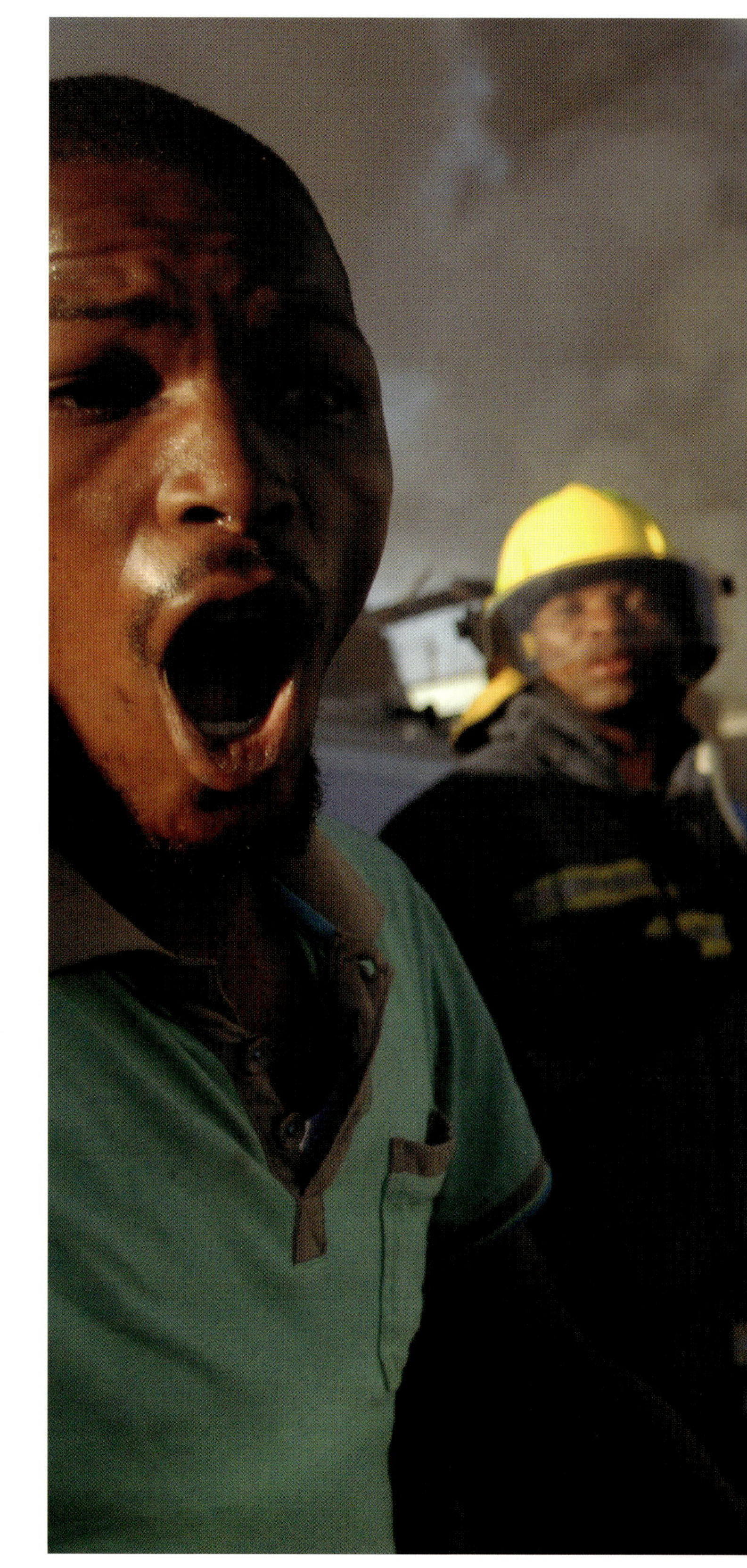

A man shouting during a horrific fire before going to work. He helped the fire fighters to quell the fire that destroyed a shack in Site C, Khayelitsha. Most of the informal dwellers in settlements burn imbalwa to keep warm, often leaving the fire unattended, which then results in fires breaking out.

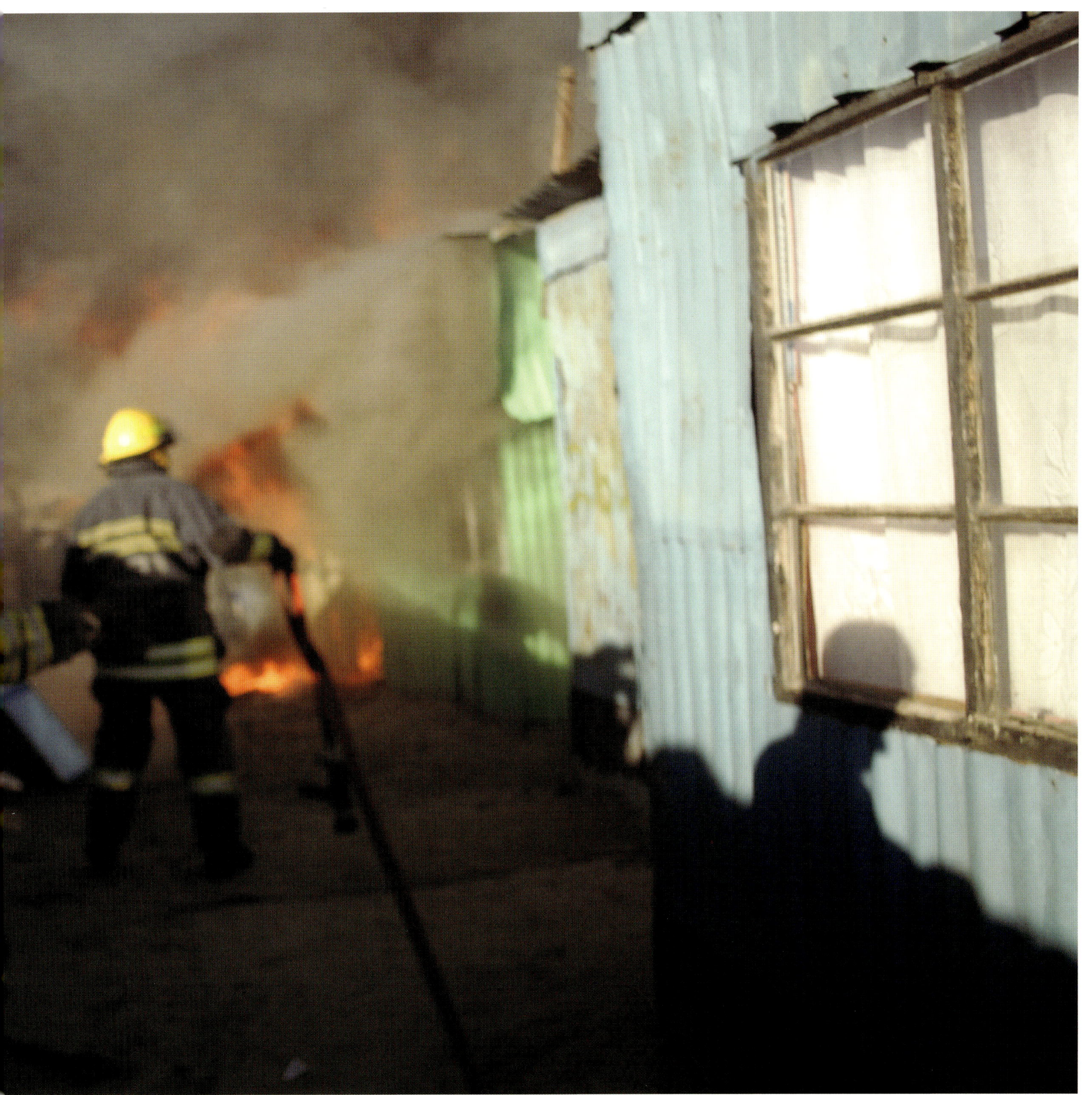

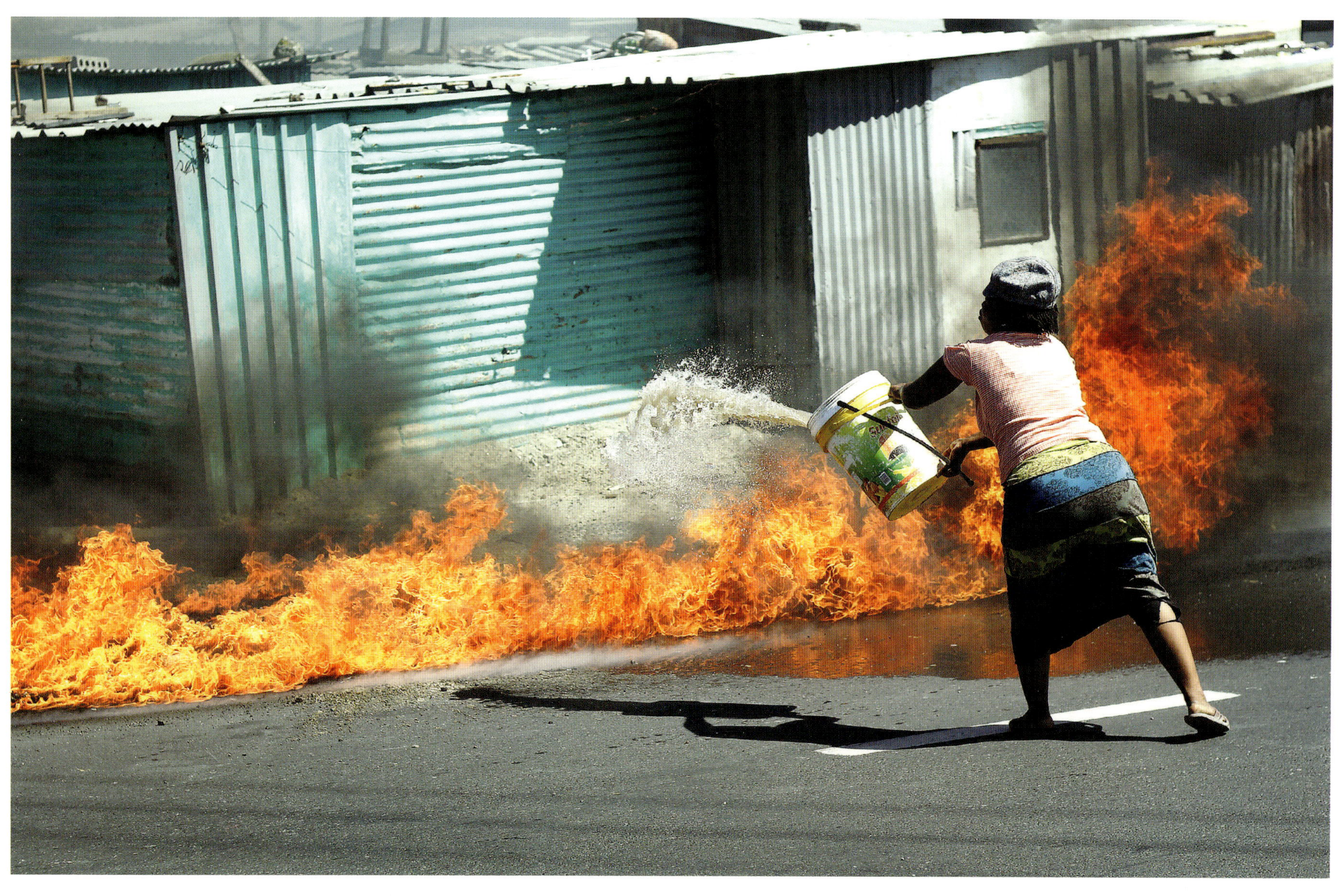

A woman attempting to put out a shack fire that is about to burn
her house down, Site C, Khayelitsha.

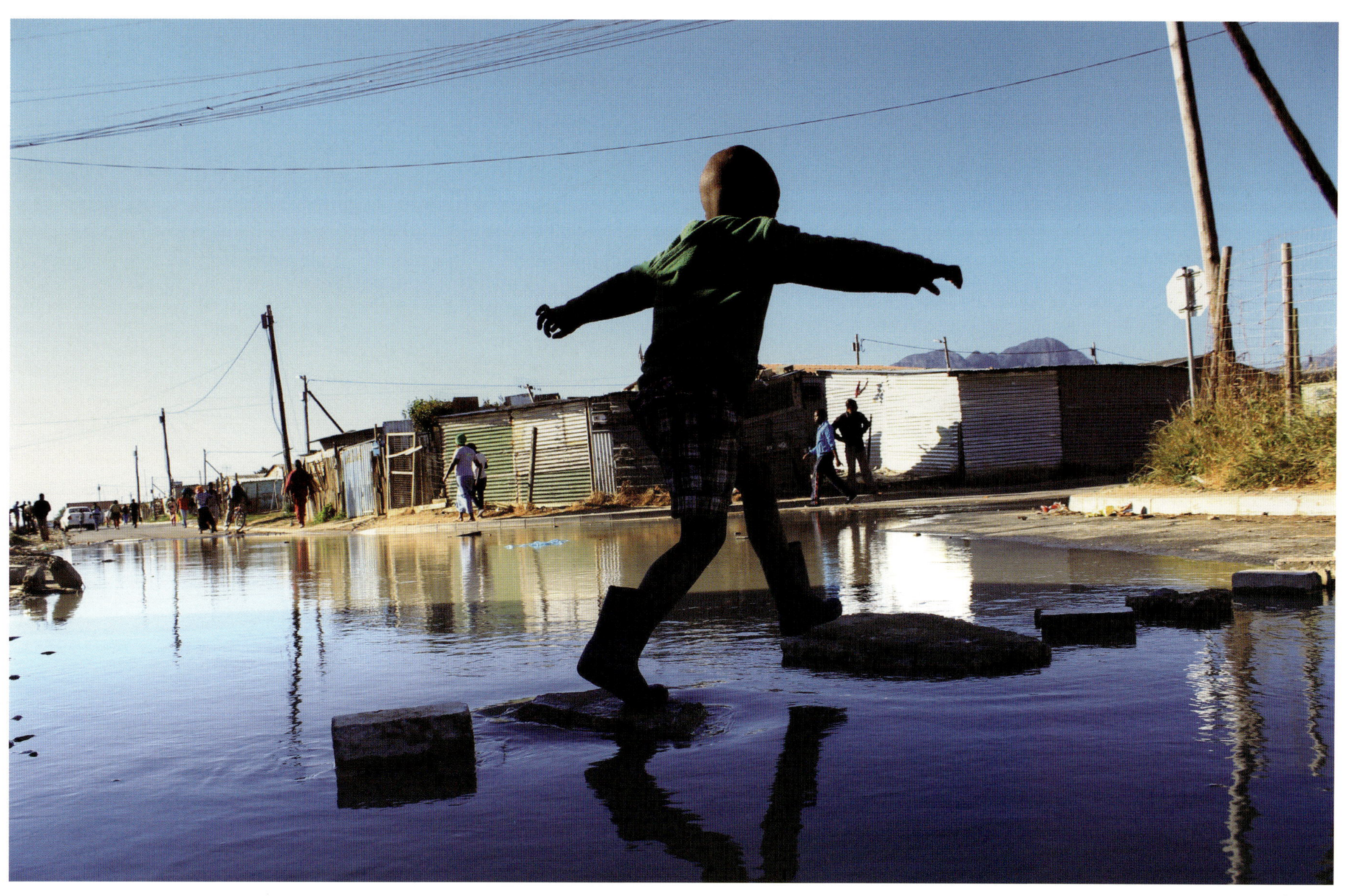

A young boy carefully choosing his path after the rain, Strand.

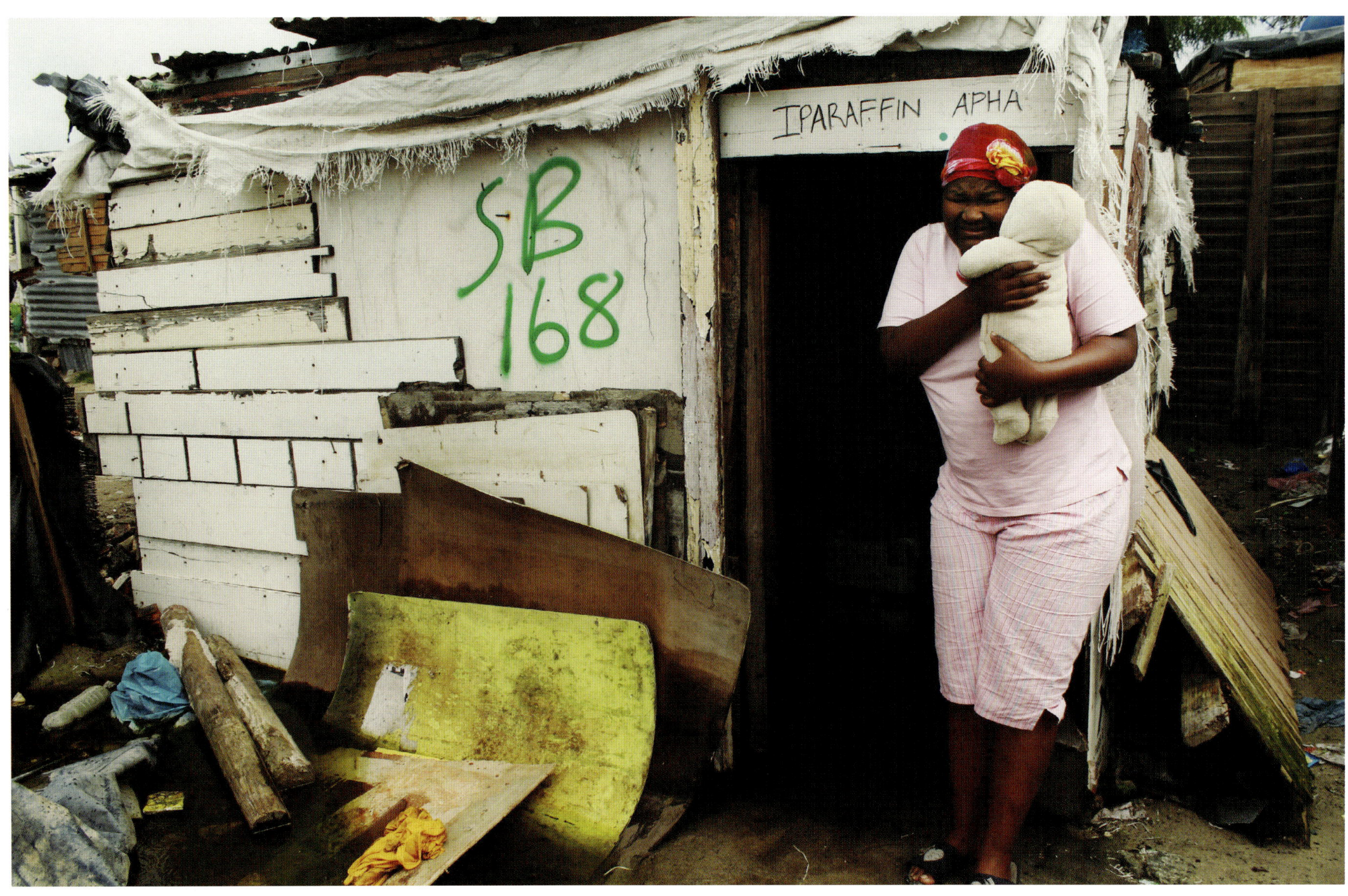

A woman and her child stand beside their flood-destroyed home
in Siqalo settlement.

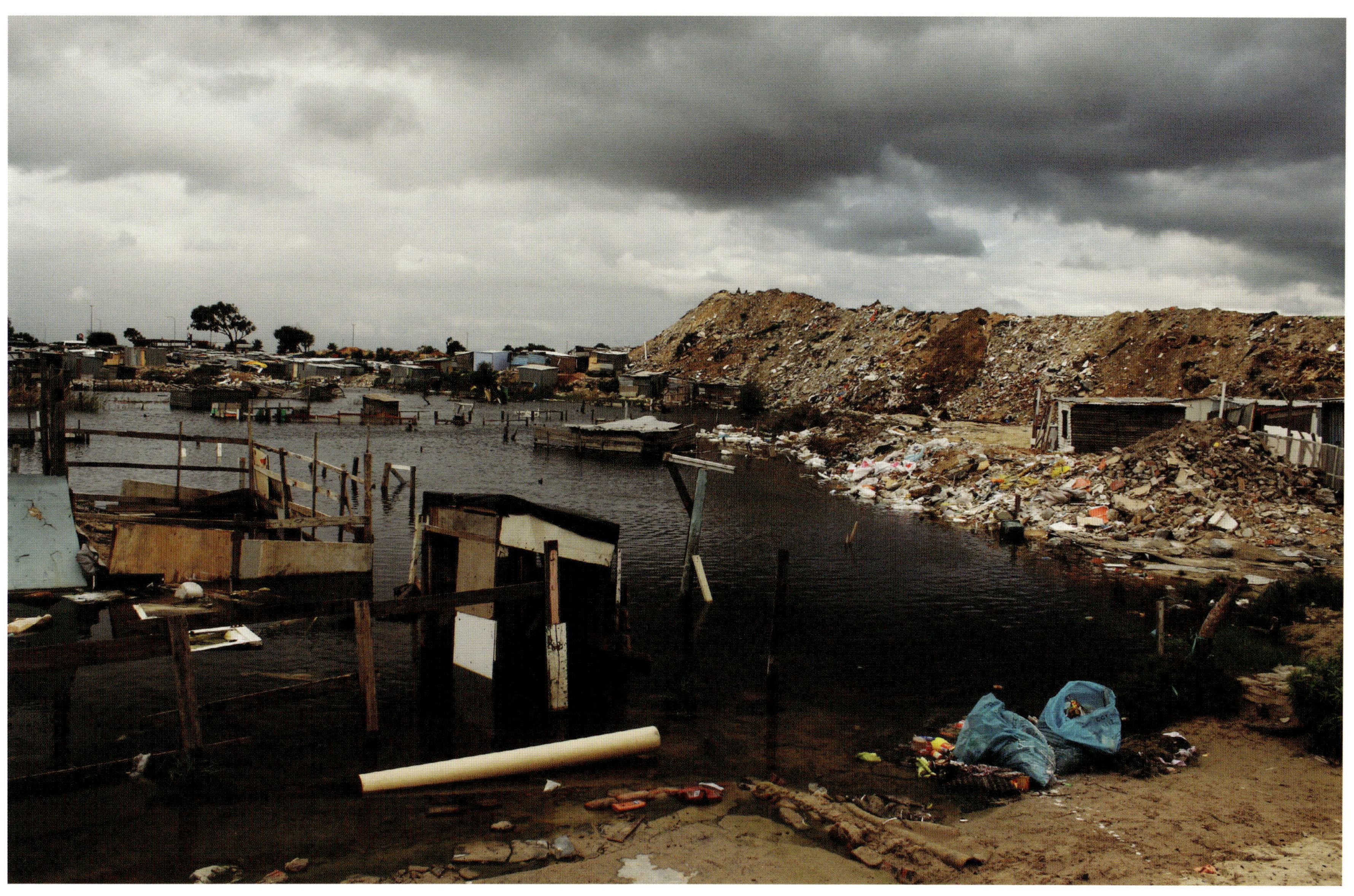

Flood-destroyed shacks, Philippi.

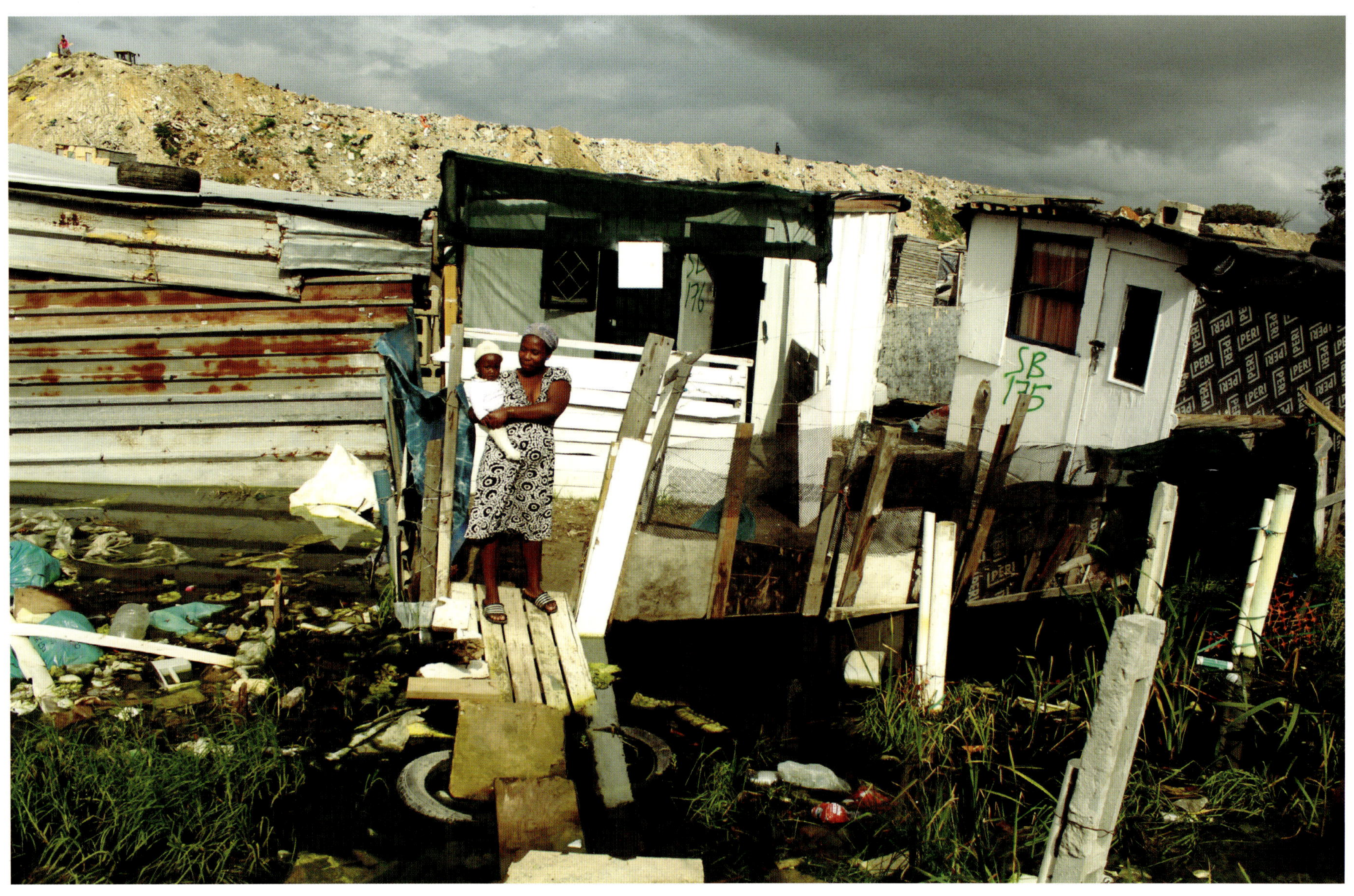

The aftermath of a flood that left many houses empty. The community blamed a construction company that made things worse by dumping rubble in and around their environment, Siqalo settlement, Philippi.

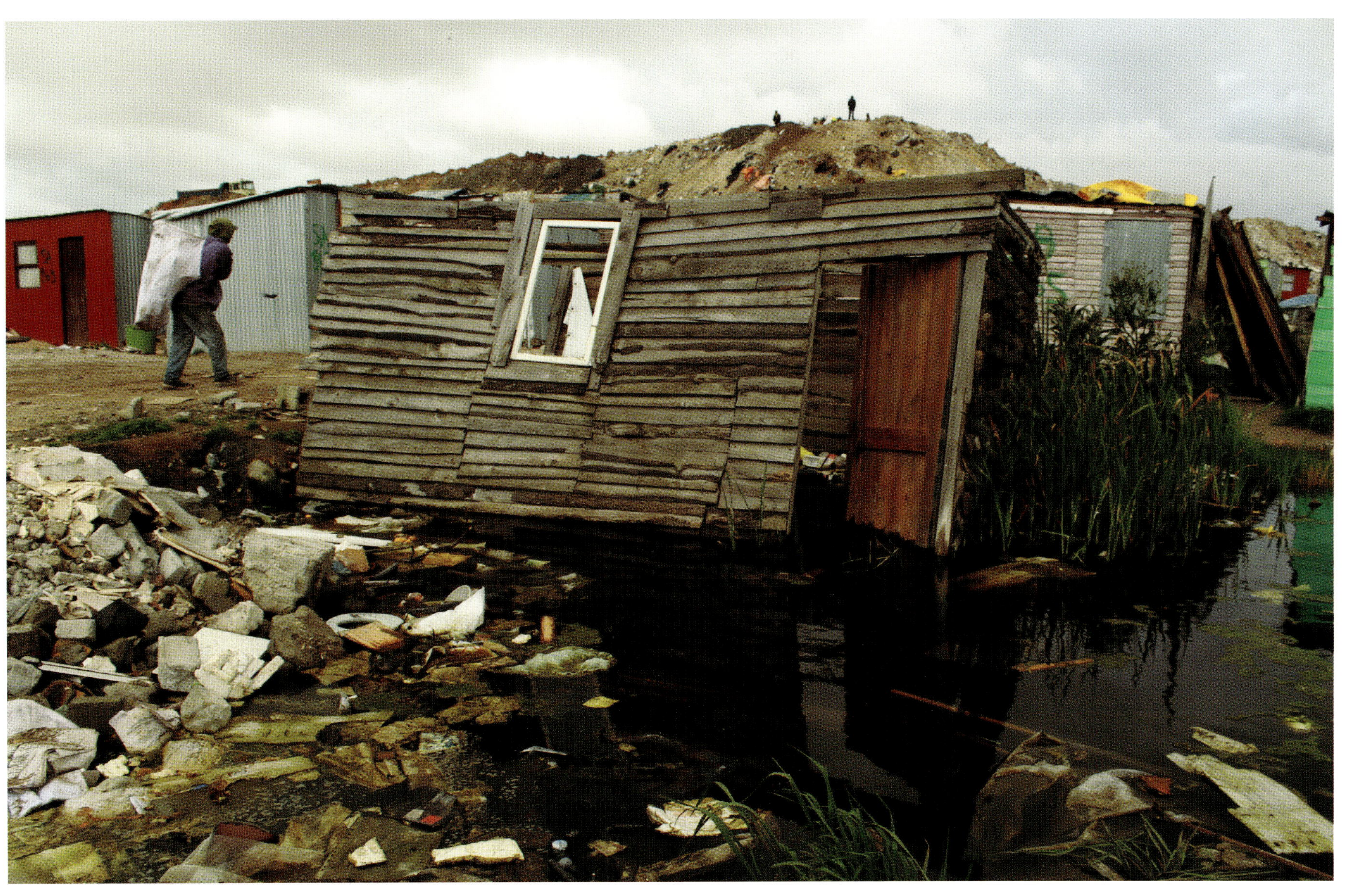

Some of the stronger shacks are only partially destroyed by floods, Philippi.

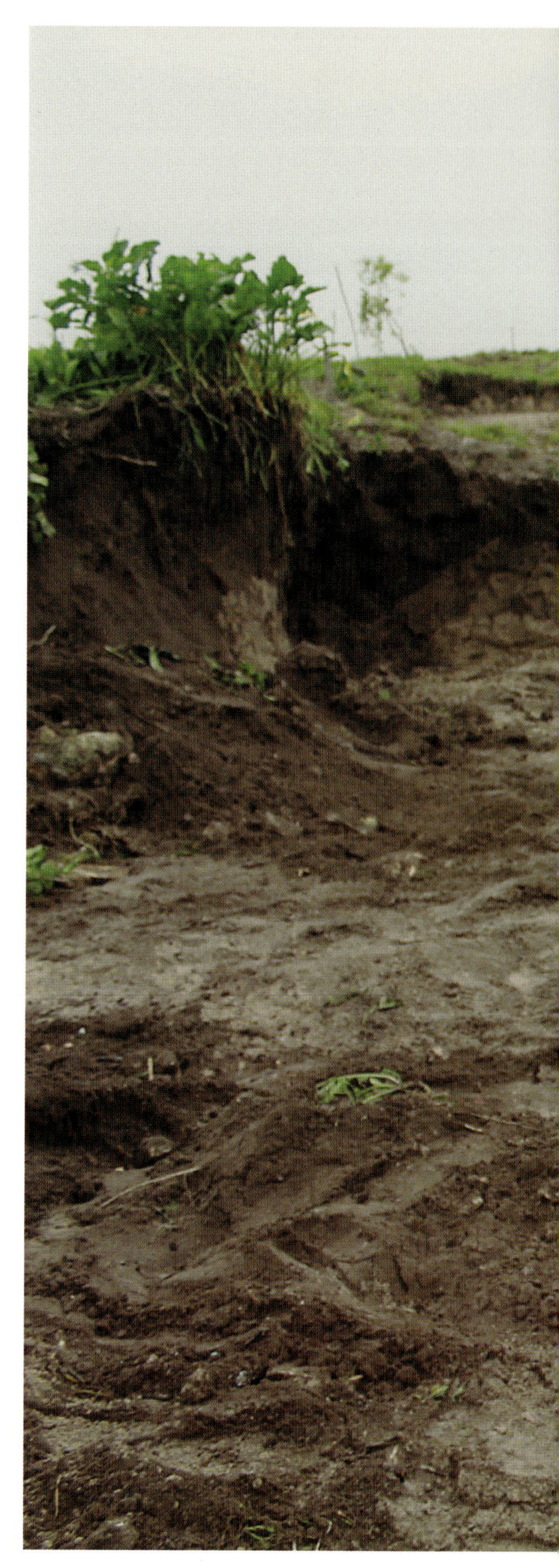

Family preparing space to forcefully occupy privately owned land in
Philippi. A court case regarding occupation and eviction is still ongoing.

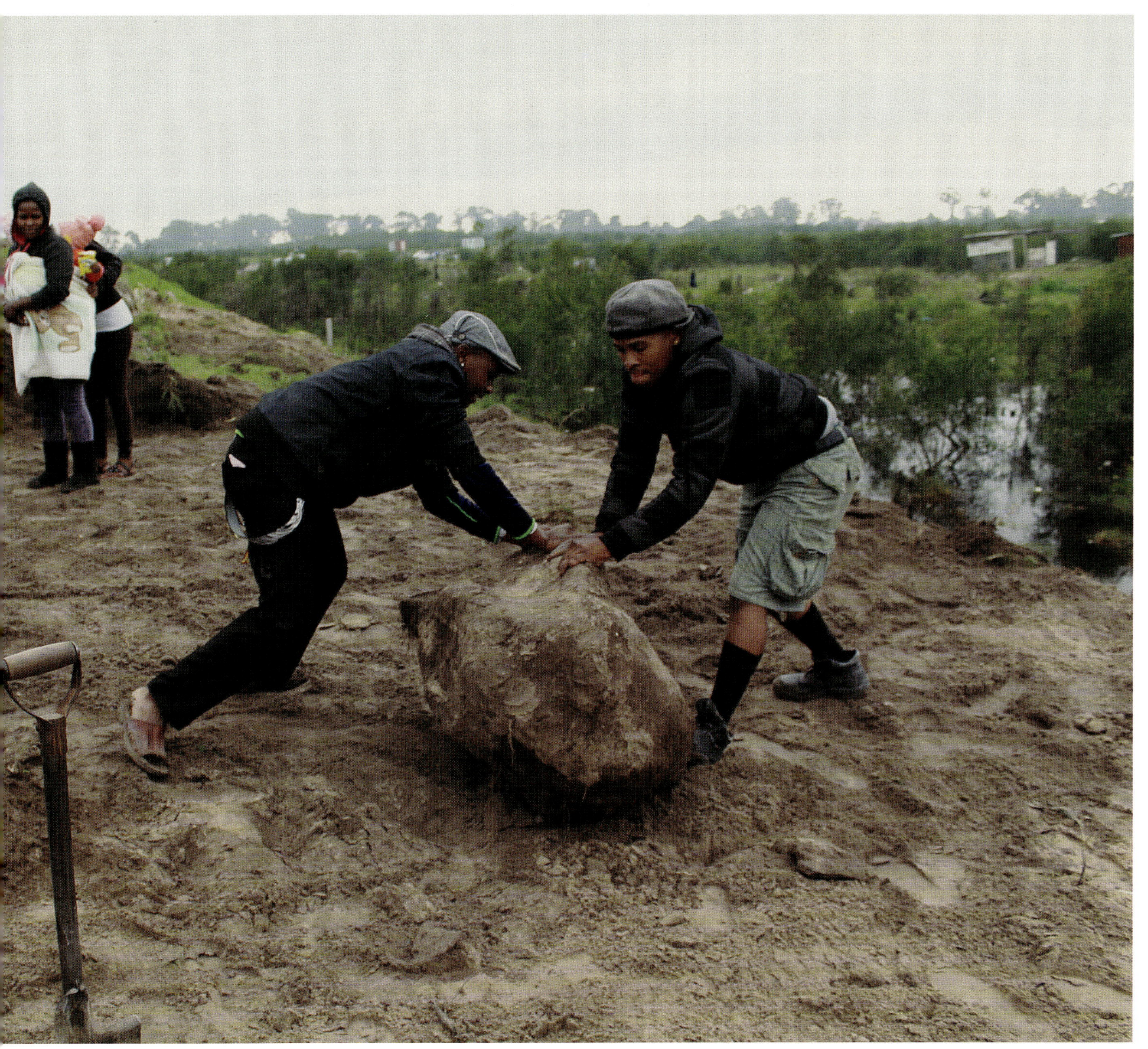

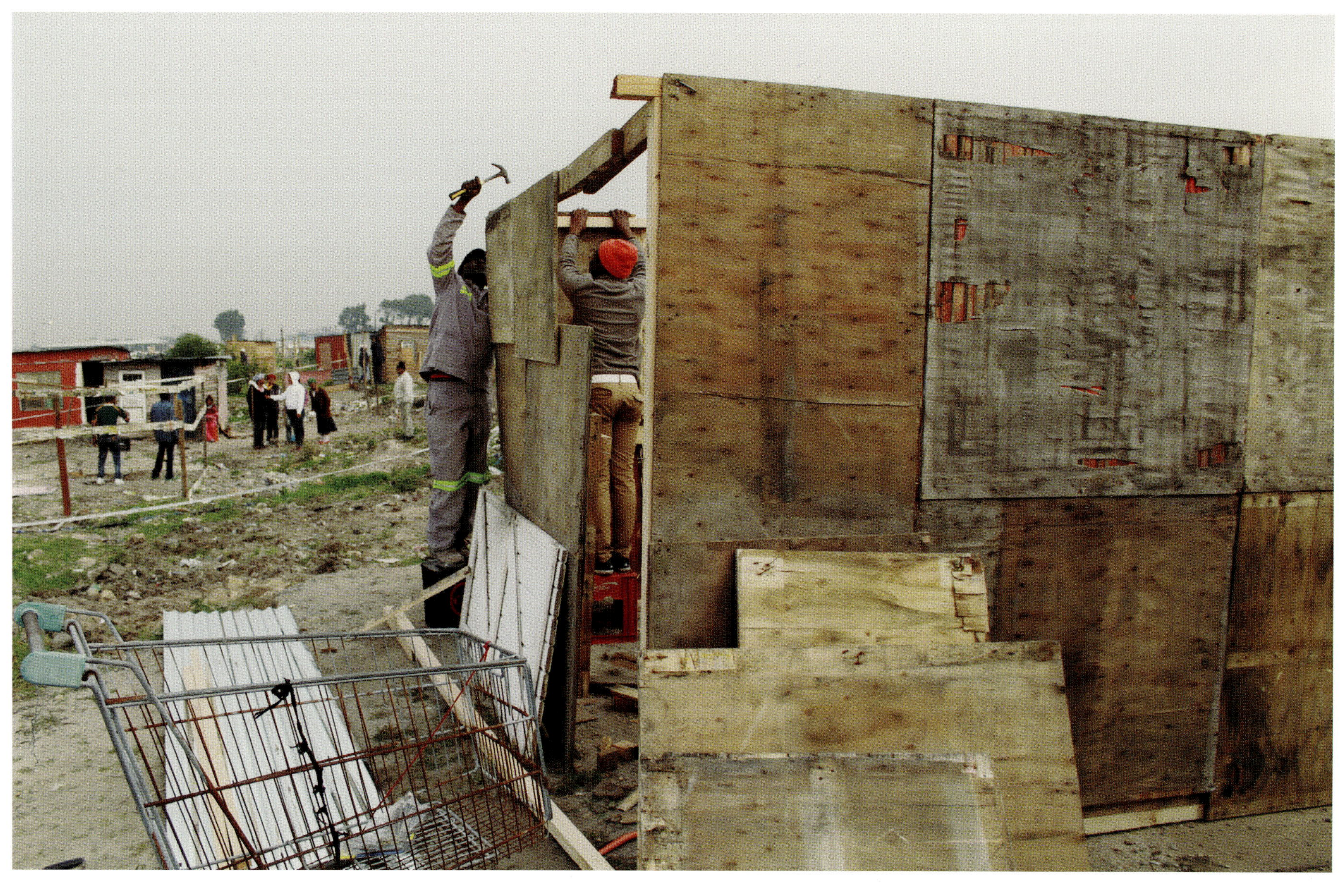

A family deconstructs their home before eviction from privately
owned land, Philippi.

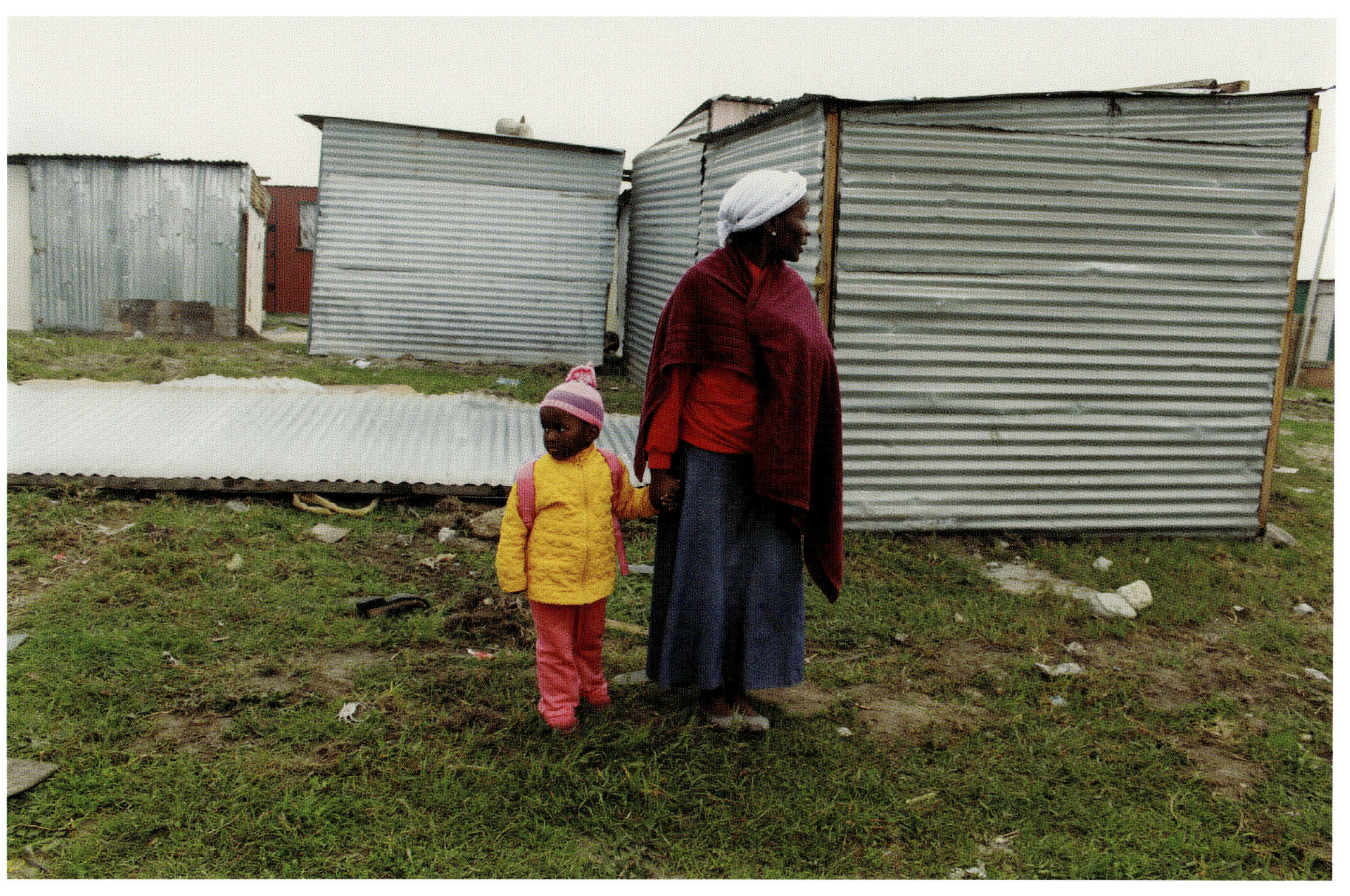

Patiently waiting for the police to evict them, Philippi.

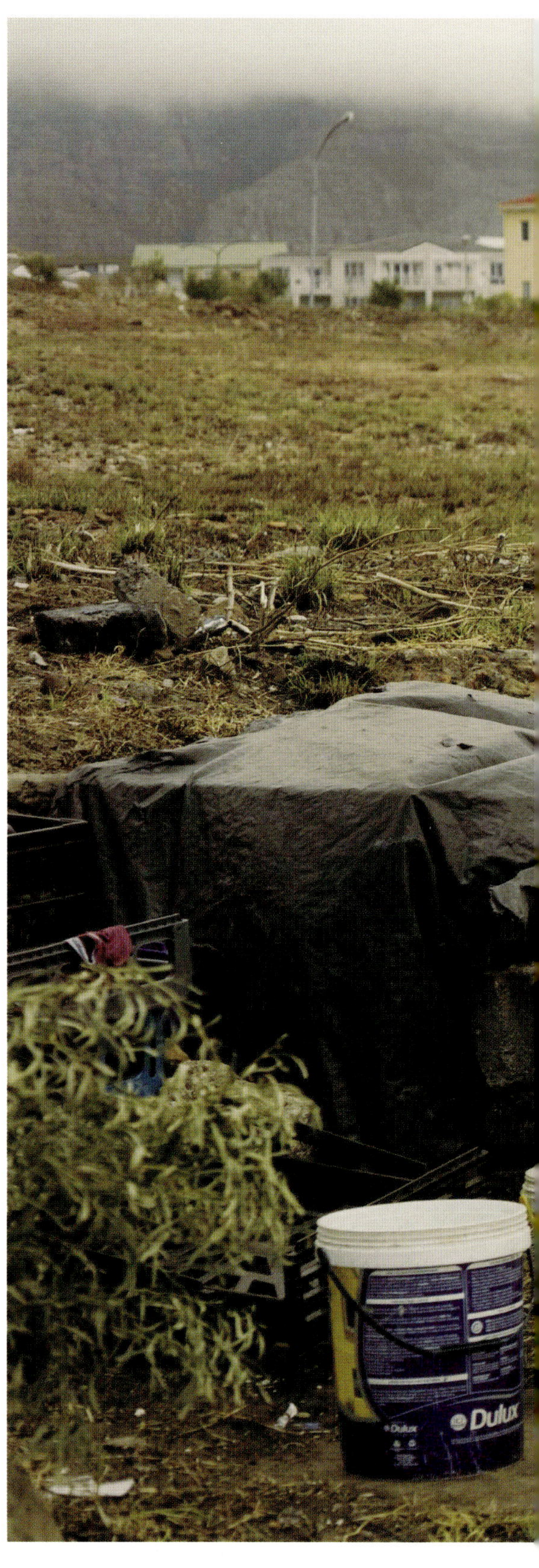

A couple evicted from a public space at the famous site that was District Six.

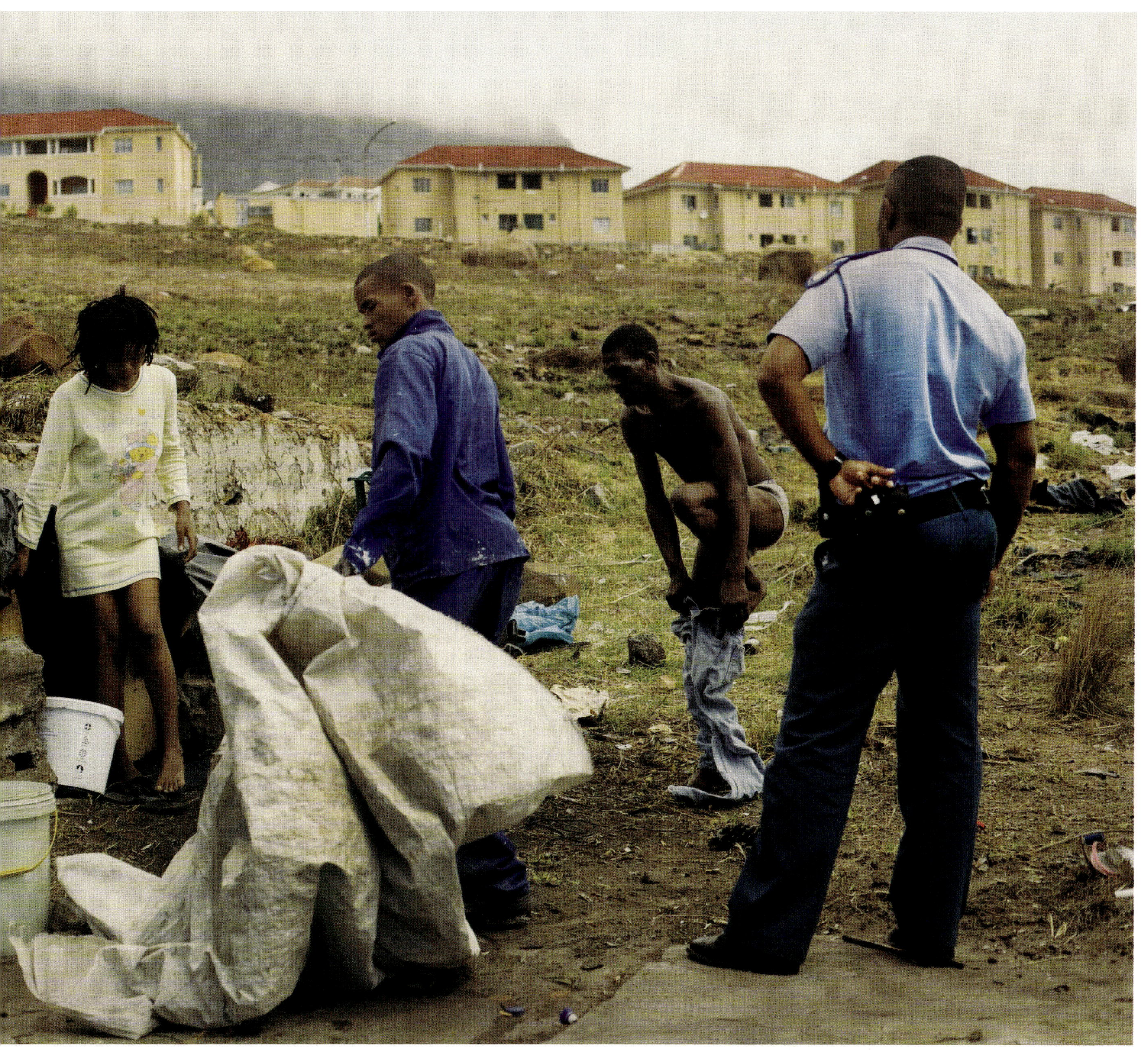

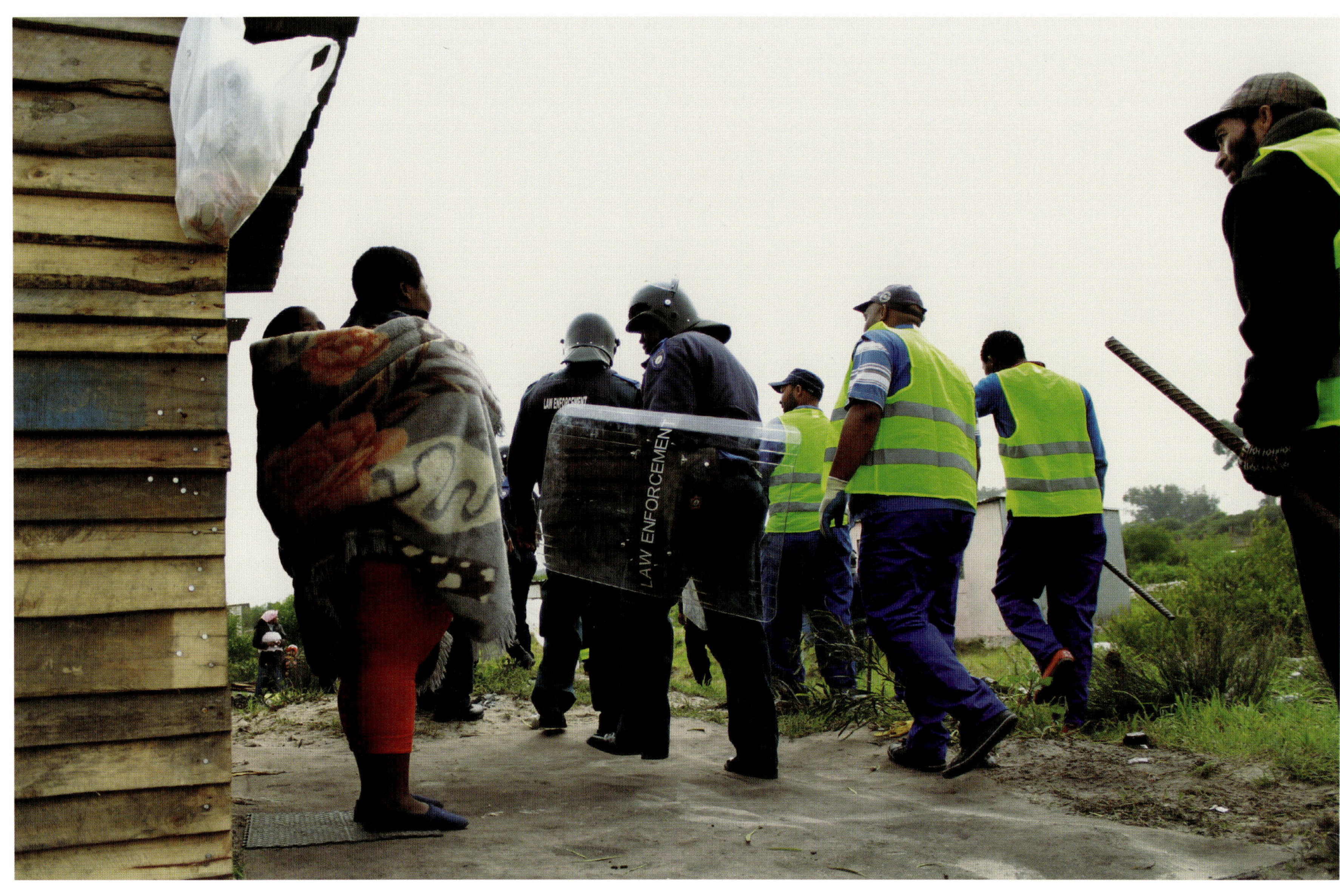

A young mother with her baby on her back, crying in front of her
demolished home on privately owned land, Marikana, Philippi.

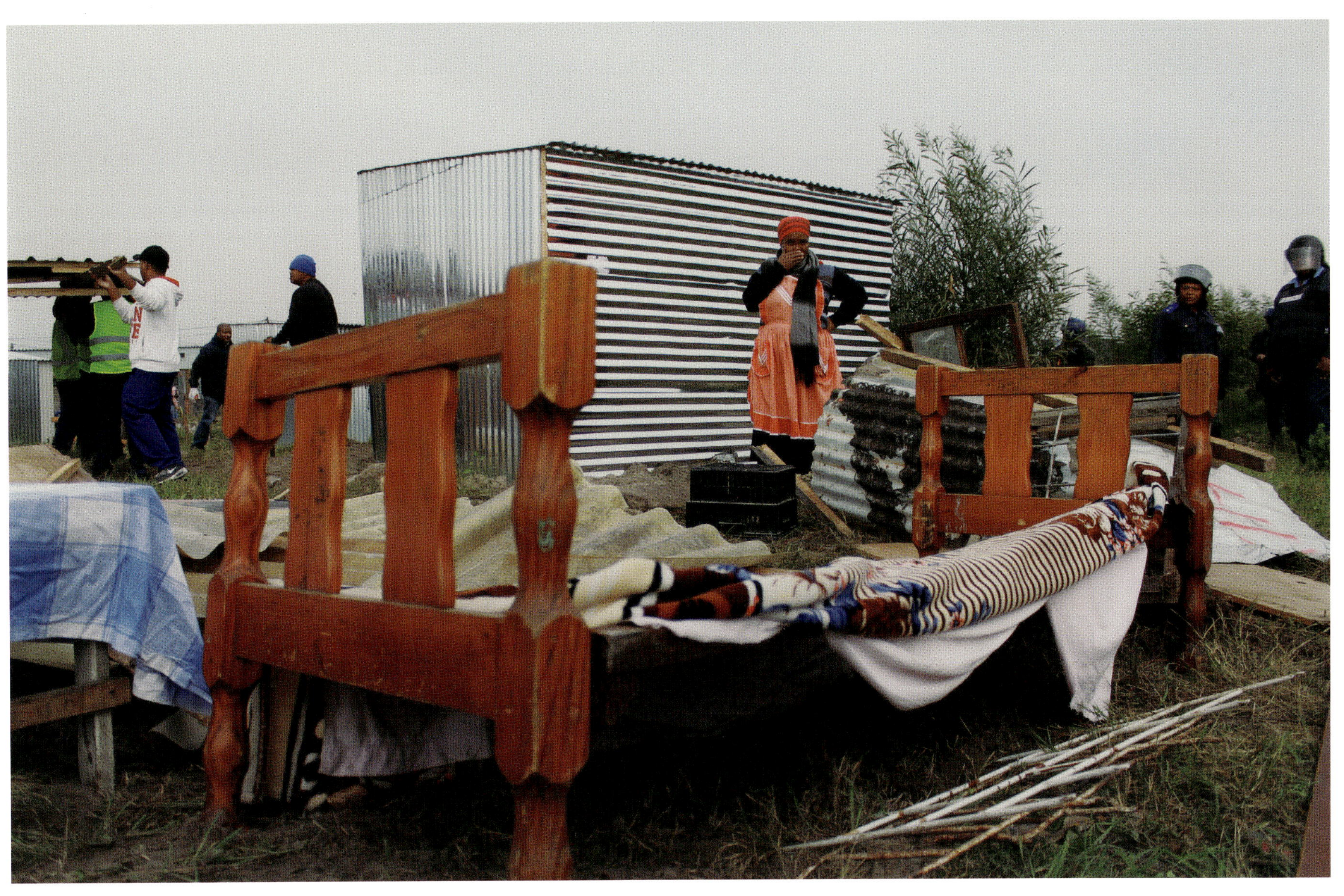

A woman looking over her broken bed. Often the little furniture
people have is damaged during evictions, Marikana, Philippi.

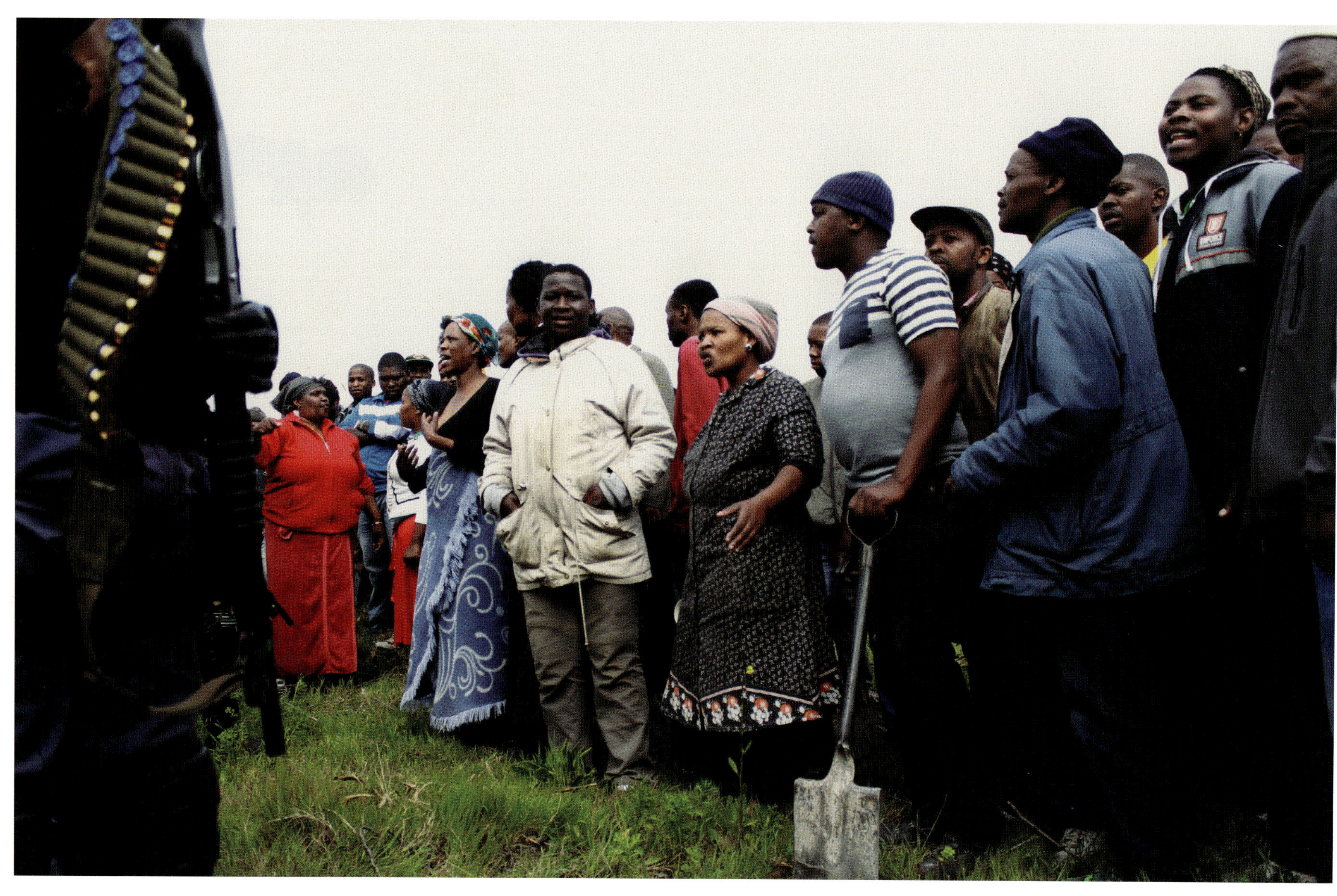

Community members confronting police trying to evict them from private land.

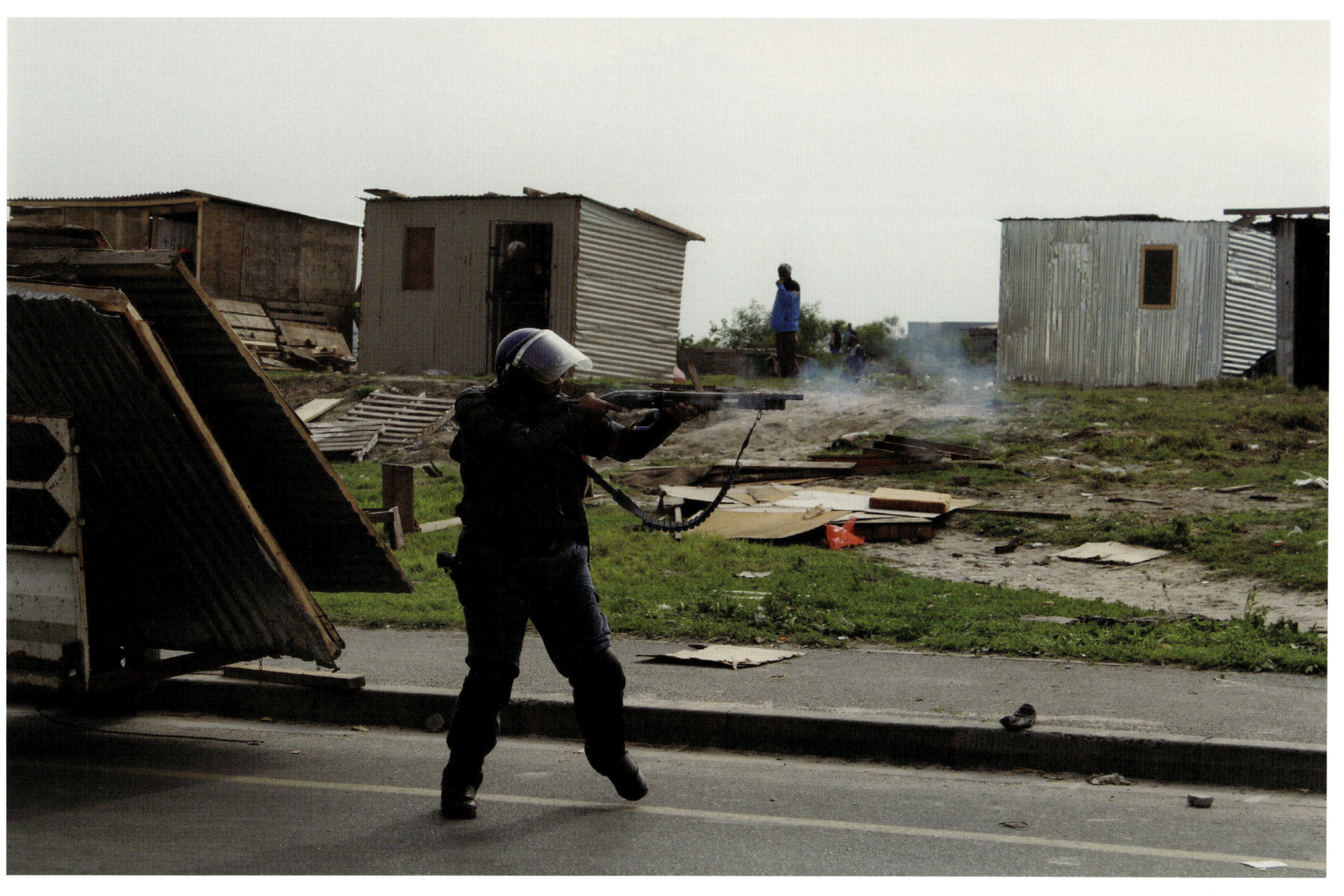

Police shoot at community members after they resist eviction, Marikana, Philippi.

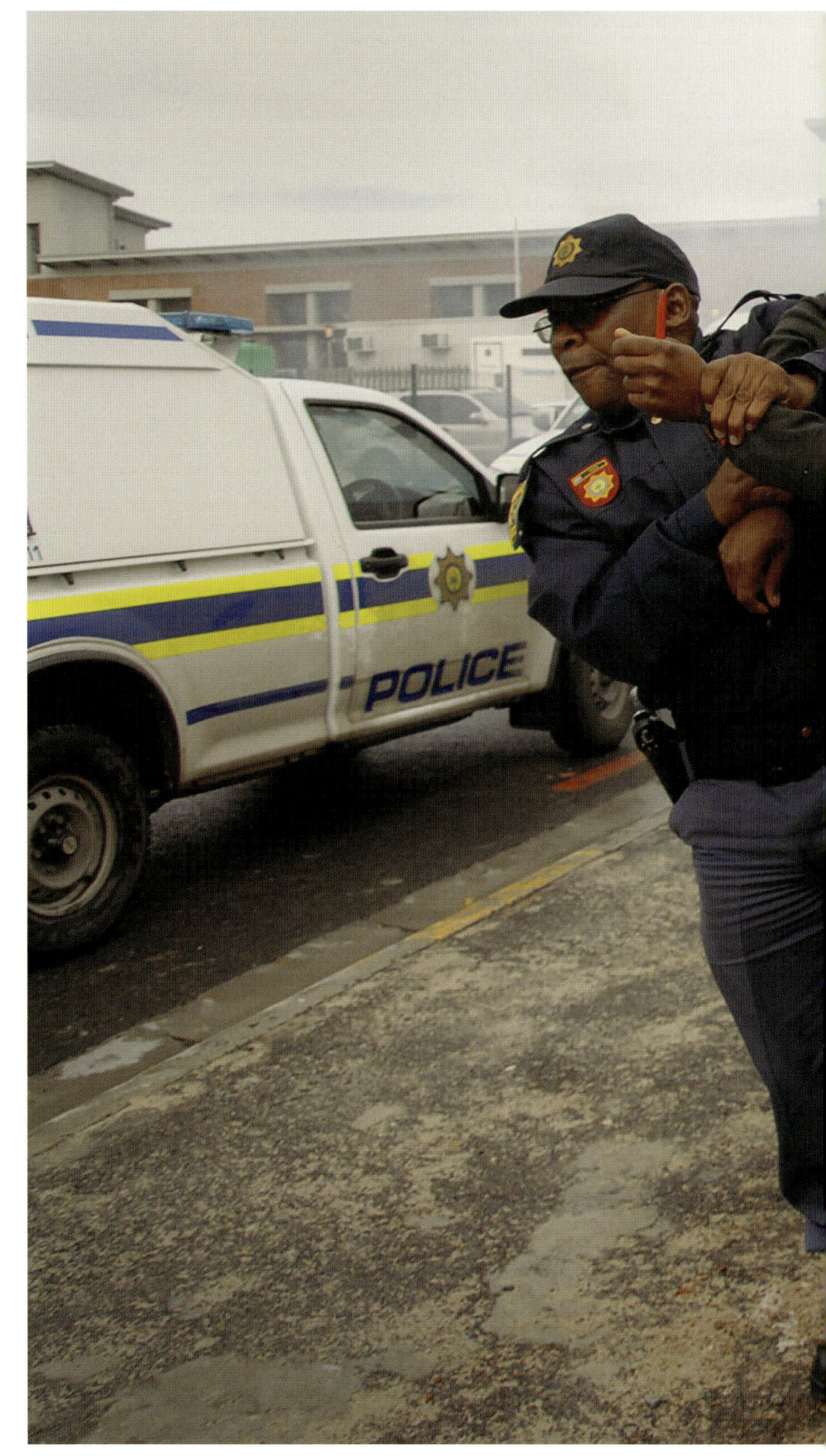

Violence erupts as community members disrupt a meeting organised by the Democratic Alliance in Harare, Khayelitsha to discuss better service delivery.

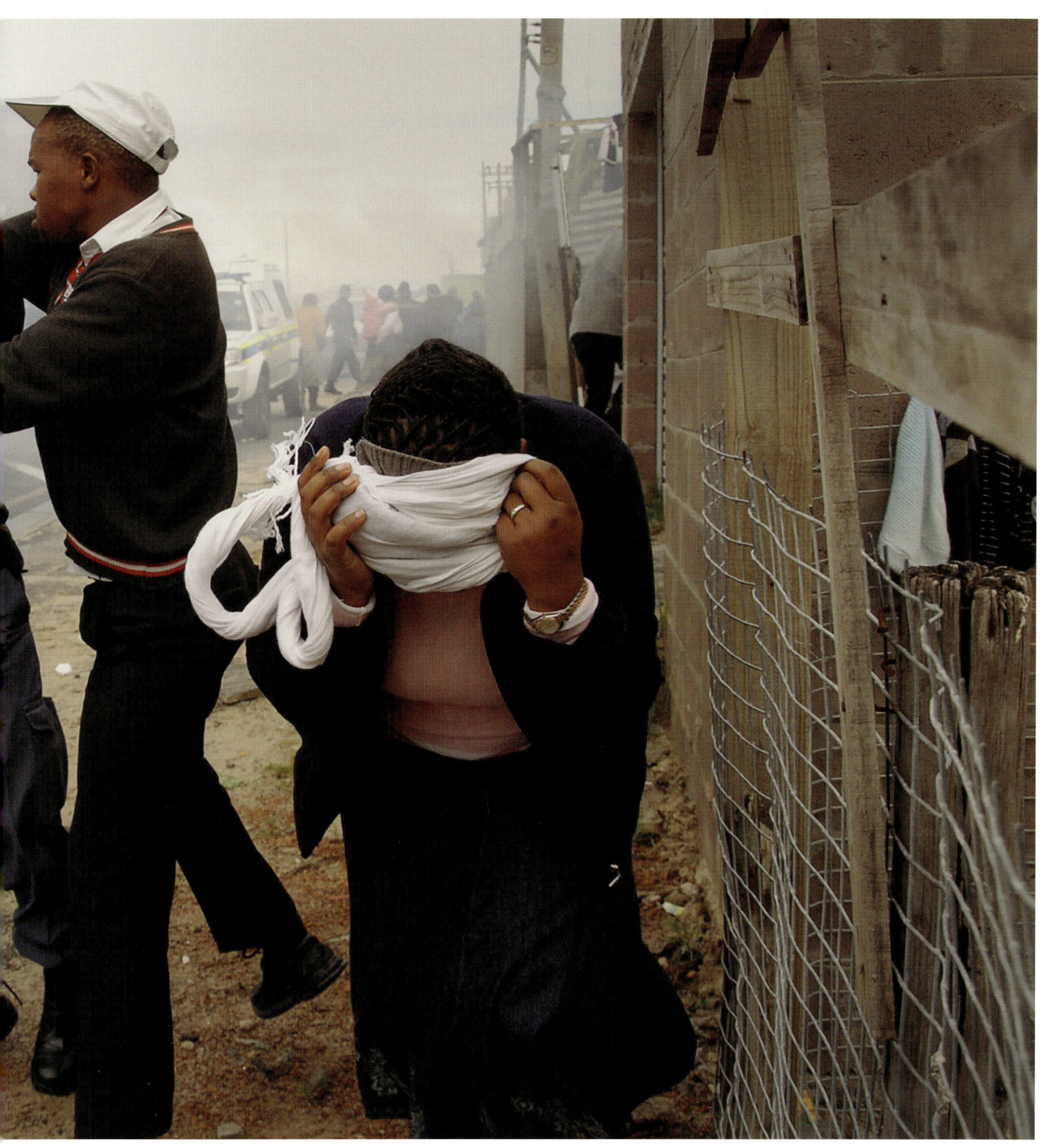

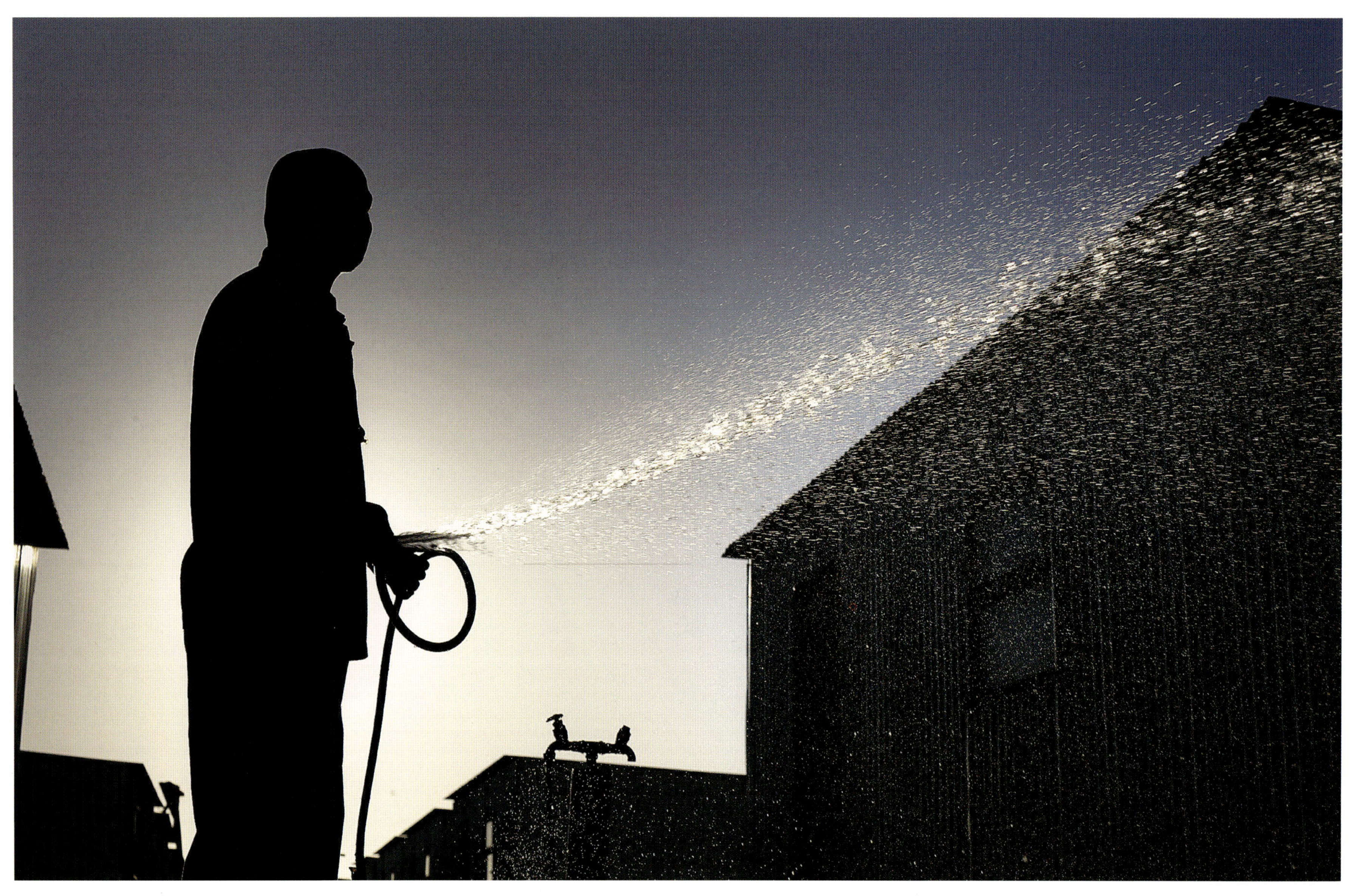

A man washes away public refuse from his premises, Khayelitsha.

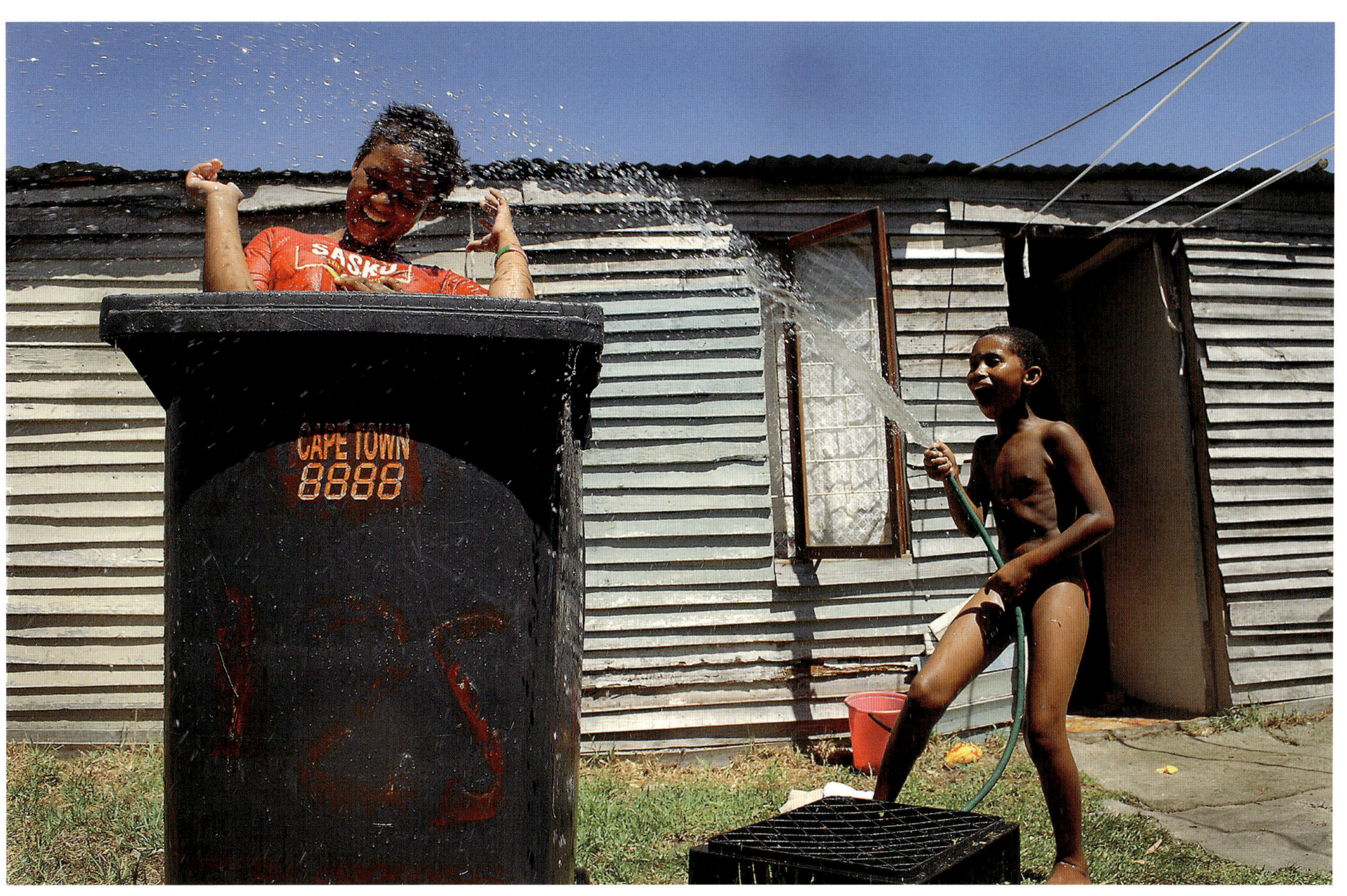

Veronique and Jason playing with water.

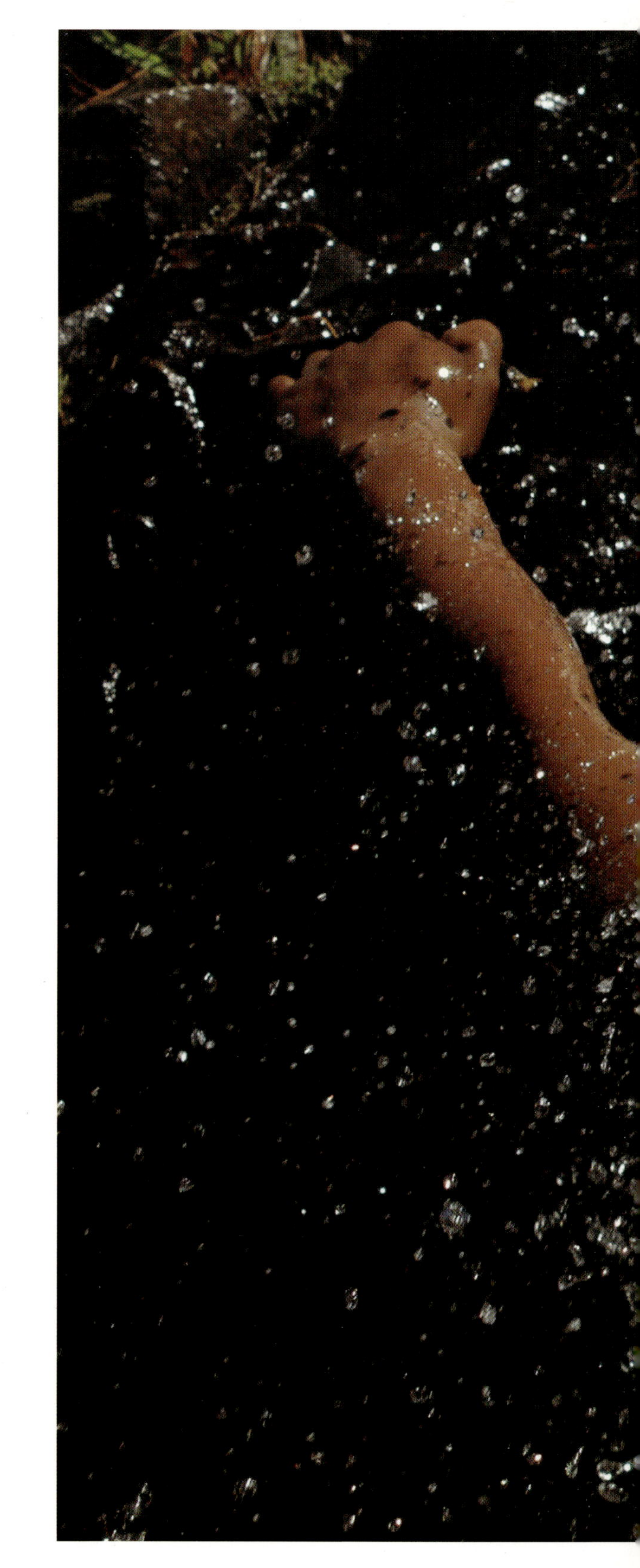

A Rastafarian participates in a ceremonial cleansing at a waterfall in Dear Park, Cape Town. Many religious groups visit this site as they claim this is the only place with pure, uncontaminated water.

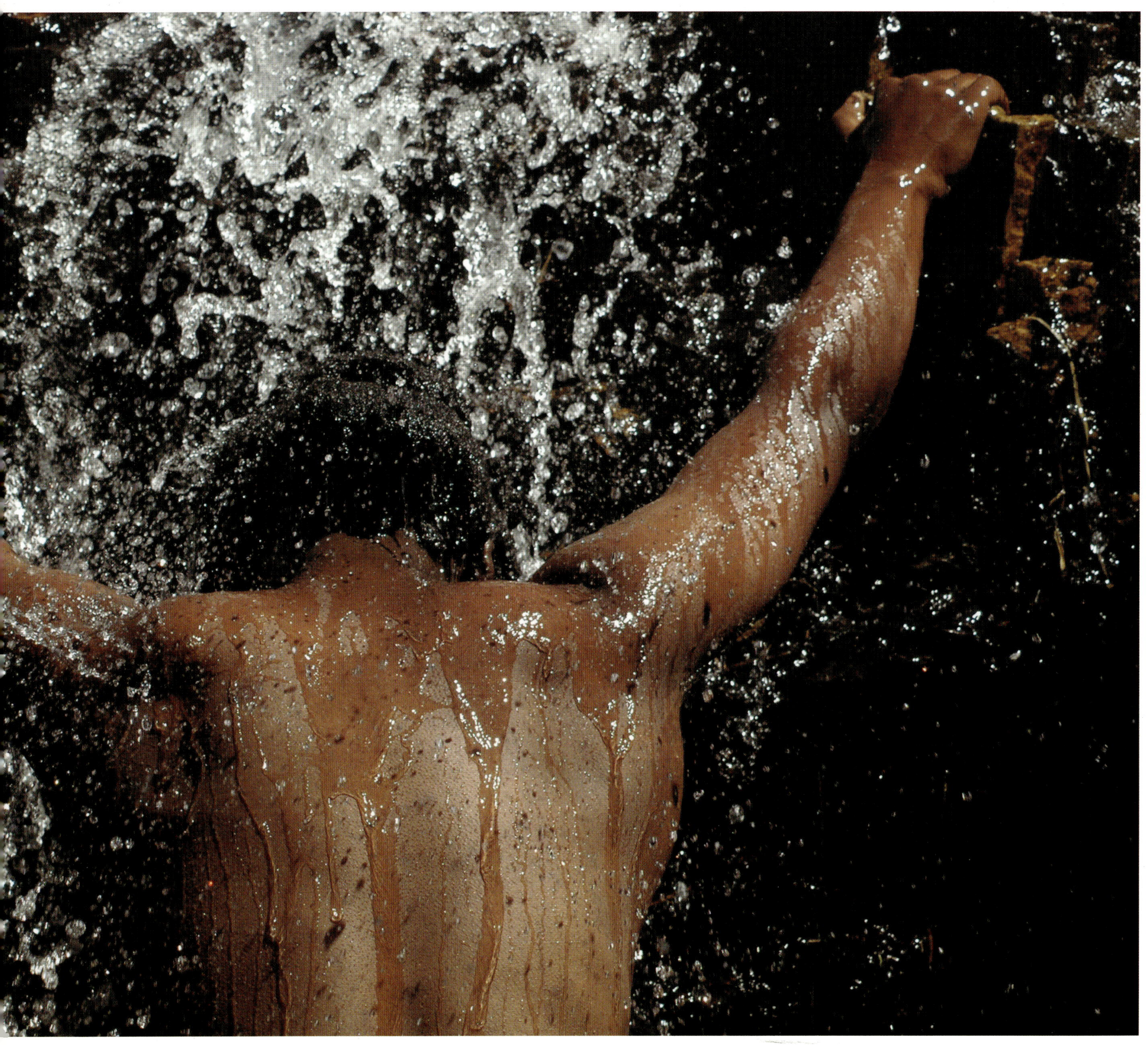

MASIXOLE FENI WAS BORN in 1987 in Cape Town. He grew up in Sakhumzi orphanage down the road from where he currently lives in the Mfuleni settlement near Khayelitsha. Feni was introduced to photography at a young age by the late Garth Stead and the Icon Photography Group, and through Jenny Altschuler's 1999 Drumming Photography workshops at the Iziko SA museum.

While still in high school he started freelancing for a few local news outlets, including *The Cape Times*, *The Argus* and GroundUp. In 2010 Feni became a full-time trainee at the SA Centre for Photography on Altschuler's informal photography programme, receiving critique and polishing his practice: shooting, editing, writing and post-producing.

Troubled by the sensational reporting around service delivery protests in townships he was inspired to challenge the linear view media takes in their reposting. For the last few years Feni has been documenting the water and sanitation conditions around him. As a 'backyard dweller' himself, Feni brings a new sensitivity to issues around service delivery.

THE ERNEST COLE Photographic Award initiated at the University of Cape Town and now part of the Centre for African Studies offers a unique opportunity for photographers to complete an existing project. The award, named after documentary photographer Ernest Cole, has been made possible by the generous support of the Peter Brown, Gavin Relly Educational and Kirsch Family Trusts, ORMS, Kier Schuringa, and the John Liebenberg Hip Op Fund.

Ernest Cole was born in South Africa in 1940 and received his first camera as a gift from a clergyman. Before leaving South Africa in the mid-'60s he worked as a photojournalist for *Drum* magazine, sharing a darkroom and friendship with the photographer Struan Robertson. On his own initiative, Cole undertook a comprehensive photographic essay in which he showed what it meant to be black under apartheid. Out of this came the book *The House of Bondage*, which was published in New York in 1967 and immediately banned in South Africa. He never returned to South Africa and died in exile in New York in 1990.

Cole was a courageous documentarian who at times risked his life to share his imagery with the world. 'He wasn't just brave. He wasn't just enterprising. He was a supremely fine photographer,' said David Goldblatt, the renowned South African photographer.

The Ernest Cole Photographic Award has been established to stimulate in-depth photography in South Africa, with an emphasis on creative responses to South African society, with preference being given to people living within the country. The purpose of the award is to support the realisation of a significant body of work with which the photographer has been engaged.

For more information, please see www.ernestcoleaward.uct.ac.za

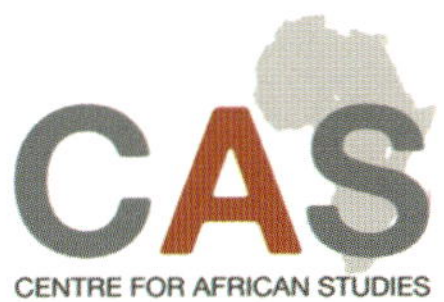

First published by Jacana Media (Pty) Ltd in 2017

10 Orange Street
Sunnyside
Auckland Park 2092
South Africa
+2711 628 3200
www.jacana.co.za

All photographs were taken between 2013 and 2016
Photographic editor: Paul Weinberg
Cover quote: Nelson Mandela, used with kind permission
   from the Nelson Mandela Foundation

ISBN 978-1-4314-2552-5

Design by Shawn Paikin
Set in Stempel Garamond 10/15pt & Univers Light 8/9.6pt
Printed by Hansa and bound by Graphicraft (PTY) LTD
Job no. 003025

See a complete list of Jacana titles at www.jacana.co.za